A DIRECTOR'S GUIDE

Duties, Liabilities and Company Law

A DIRECTOR'S GUIDE

Duties, Liabilities and Company Law

by

Colin McArthur

Ian Barnard

Solicitors of the Supreme Court

Both of Field Fisher Waterhouse

WATERLOW PUBLISHERS

First edition 1990

© Colin McArthur and Ian Barnard 1990

Waterlow Publishers
24 Gray's Inn Road
London
WC1X 8HR

A division of Pergamon Professional and Financial Services PLC

All rights reserved. No part of this publication may be reproduced, stored in a retrieval system, or transmitted, in any form or by any means, electronic, mechanical or photocopying, recording or otherwise, without the prior permission of Waterlow Publishers.

Care has been taken in the preparation of this publication and no responsibility for loss occasioned to any person acting or refraining from action as a result of any material in this publication can be accepted by the authors or publishers.

ISBN 0 08 040121 X

British Library Cataloguing in Publication Data
McArthur, Colin
   A director's guide: duties, liabilities and company law.
   1. Great Britain. Companies. Directors. Law. Obligations
   I. Title   II. Barnard, Ian
   344.1066642

Printed in Great Britain by
BPCC Wheatons Ltd, Exeter, Devon

PREFACE

Company directors undertake a wide range of duties and responsibilities, and as certain recent publicised court cases have emphasised, directors can face considerable personal liability, both under the civil law and the criminal law. The trend appears to be to expect higher standards of directors, and it is important therefore that directors should have a clear understanding of their responsibilities.

The aim of this book is to explain the role, duties and responsibilities of directors and to highlight particularly the "danger areas" where directors can face personal liability. At the same time the book aims to cover the rules governing how a limited company should operate.

As a result of consolidating legislation, the main provisions of company legislation are now contained in the Companies Act 1985, and those relating to insolvency are contained in the Insolvency Act 1986. However in November 1989, a new Companies Act was passed which amends the law in a number of important respects. The Companies Act 1989 will be brought into force in stages over the next 15 months or so, but the precise dates are not yet known. Throughout the text we have referred to the Companies Act 1989 and drawn attention to the provisions which will be coming into force. Otherwise, the law is stated as at February 1990.

Finally, we have referred throughout the book to the "standard articles" or to what articles normally state – these are references to the 1985 Table A articles. Many companies' articles will still follow earlier versions of Table A, and it is always important to check the company's own articles. For reference, a summary of the main provisions of the 1985 Table A (with corresponding provisions of the 1948 Table A) is set out in Appendix A.

Colin McArthur and Ian Barnard

Field Fisher Waterhouse

Contents

		Page
Preface		v
Contents		vii

1 Points to consider before becoming a director		1
1.1	The nature of a limited company	1
1.2	The responsibilities of a director	1
1.3	Independence	2
1.4	Time	2
1.5	Information	2
1.6	Qualifications	2
1.7	Restrictions	3
1.8	Conflicts	3
1.9	Memorandum and articles of association	3
1.10	Latest audited accounts	4
1.11	Listed companies and their subsidiaries	4
1.12	Shareholders' agreement	4

2 How a limited company operates		5
2.1	Distinguishing features of a limited company	5
2.2	How a limited company is formed	5
2.3	The memorandum of association	6
2.4	The articles of association	7
2.5	Types of limited company	7
2.6	Safeguards for third parties	8
2.7	Relationship between shareholders and directors	10

3 Who and what is a director		11
3.1	Role of a director	11
3.2	Who is a director	12
3.3	Shadow directors	12
3.4	Alternate directors	13
3.5	General duties of a director	13
3.6	Number of directors	14

		Page
4 Appointment of directors		15
4.1	How appointments are made	15
4.2	Checklist of steps to be taken	15
4.3	Employment contract	16
5 Directors' detailed duties – general duties		17
5.1	General	17
5.2	Care and skill	17
5.3	Attending board meetings: time and attention	19
5.4	Delegation: responsibility for acts of others	20
5.5	Duty not to exceed powers	21
5.6	Duty to have regard to the interests of employees	21
5.7	Duty to creditors	22
5.8	Duty to consumers or the community	22
5.9	Statutory obligations	22
6 Directors' detailed duties – fiduciary duties		23
6.1	General	23
6.2	Duty to act in the best interests of the company	23
6.3	Duty not to exercise powers for a collateral purpose	25
6.4	Duty not to compete	25
6.5	Duty of confidentiality	26
6.6	Duty to disclose interests	26
6.7	Duty not to make secret profits	26
6.8	Duty not to misapply company assets	26
6.9	Nominee directors	27
7 Relief from liability		28
7.1	General	28
7.2	Relief from liability by court	28
7.3	Exemption from liability in articles or by contract	29
7.4	Settlement of claim	29
7.5	Ratification	29
7.6	Insurance	30
8 Directors' meetings		31
8.1	The need for meetings	31
8.2	Written resolutions	31
8.3	Frequency of meetings	32

		Page
8.4	General conduct of board meetings	33
8.5	Notice of meetings	33
8.6	Quorum	33
8.7	Difficulty obtaining a quorum	34
8.8	Chairman	34
8.9	Decisions	35
8.10	Voting where director has an interest	35
8.11	Minutes of meetings	35
8.12	Circulation of minutes	37
8.13	Committees and delegation	37
8.14	Dissent	37

9 Directors' powers   39

9.1	Power of the board generally	39
9.2	Limitation of directors' powers	39
9.3	Board exceeding their own powers or the powers of the company	40
9.4	Power of an individual director	41
9.5	Statutory protection given to third parties dealing with a company	42
9.6	Misuse of directors' powers	44
9.7	Gratuitous transactions	44
9.8	Dividends	45
9.9	Borrowing and charges	46
9.10	Bank accounts and cheques	47

10 Directors' disclosure of interests   48

10.1	General	48
10.2	Disclosure of interests	48
10.3	General interests	49
10.4	Nature of interests which need to be disclosed	49
10.5	Effect of disclosure of interest	50
10.6	Ratification by shareholders	50

11 Arrangements between directors and the company which are subject to restriction   51

11.1	General	51
11.2	Service contracts	51
11.3	Loans to directors	53
11.4	Substantial property transactions	55
11.5	Compensation for loss of office	56

	Page
12 Directors' share interests and dealings	58
12.1 Notification of share interests in the company	58
12.2 Dealing in share options	58
12.3 Insider dealing	59
13 Directors' remuneration, pension and other benefits	61
13.1 General considerations	61
13.2 Directors' fees and expenses	61
13.3 Remuneration as executives	62
13.4 Pensions	63
13.5 Other benefits and expenses	65
13.6 Share schemes	65
13.7 Taxation	66
14 Directors' liabilities to third parties	67
14.1 General position	67
14.2 Contracts	67
14.3 Negligence and other "torts"	69
14.4 Criminal offences	70
14.5 Companies Act offences	71
14.6 Liability for tax	71
14.7 Guarantees	71
14.8 Bills of exchange	72
14.9 Other liabilities	72
15 Directors and insolvency	73
15.1 Introduction	73
15.2 Fraudulent trading	73
15.3 Wrongful trading	74
15.4 General precautions to take in advance	75
15.5 Steps to take when financial problems arise	76
15.6 Transactions once the company becomes "insolvent"	77
15.7 Position once liquidation inevitable	79
15.8 Liquidation	80
15.9 Misfeasance	81
15.10 Disqualification of directors	81
15.11 Restrictions on re-use of company name	81

		Page
16 Accounts, finance and taxation		83
16.1	Accounting records	83
16.2	Management accounts	83
16.3	Requirement for audited accounts	84
16.4	Time limit for laying and filing accounts	85
16.5	Auditors	86
16.6	Error in audited accounts	86
16.7	Corporation tax	87
16.8	Advance corporation tax	88
17 Administration		89
17.1	Documents and records to be available for inspection	89
17.2	Statutory books	90
17.3	Filing documents at Companies House	91
17.4	Company stationery and documents	92
17.5	Places of business	93
17.6	Company secretary	93
17.7	Company seal	94
18 Issue of shares		96
18.1	General	96
18.2	Authorised share capital	96
18.3	Types of shares	97
18.4	Authority to issue shares	97
18.5	Pre-emption rights on share issues	98
18.6	Issue of shares for cash	99
18.7	Issue of shares for non-cash consideration	100
18.8	Directors' duties in respect of share issues	101
18.9	Formalities in respect of share issues	101
18.10	Share certificates	102
19 Financial assistance for acquisition of company's own shares		103
19.1	General prohibition	103
19.2	General exceptions applying to all companies	103
19.3	Additional exceptions applying to private companies	104
19.4	Directors' liability	104

	Page
20 Purchase by a company of its own shares: redeemable shares	105
20.1 Purchase by a company of its own shares	105
20.2 Redeemable shares	106
20.3 Special provisions applying to private companies	106
20.4 Other reductions of capital	107
20.5 Tax	107
21 Transfer of shares	108
21.1 General	108
21.2 Form of transfer	108
21.3 Restrictions on transfer and pre-emption rights	108
21.4 Share certificates	109
22 Directors and shareholders	110
22.1 General duties to shareholders	110
22.2 Directors' dealings which require shareholder approval	110
22.3 Other shareholder approval	110
22.4 Circulars	110
22.5 Prospectuses	111
22.6 Takeovers	113
22.7 Minority rights	113
23 Shareholders' meetings	116
23.1 Annual general meeting	116
23.2 Annual return: filing of audited accounts	117
23.3 Extraordinary general meetings	117
23.4 Class meetings	118
23.5 Calling shareholders' meetings	118
23.6 Conduct of meetings	119
23.7 Proxies	120
23.8 Adjournments	120
23.9 Minutes of meetings	121
24 Shareholders' resolutions	122
24.1 Types of resolutions	122
24.2 Amendments to resolutions	123
24.3 Written resolutions	123

		Page
24.4	Statutory written resolutions (private companies)	124
24.5	Elective resolutions (private companies)	125

25 Litigation — 127

25.1	Outline of proceedings	127
25.2	Importance of written records	127
25.3	"Without prejudice" and "subject to contract"	127
25.4	Discovery	129
25.5	Action to take	129
25.6	Limitation of actions	130

26 Ceasing to be a director — 131

26.1	Resignation	131
26.2	Retirement by rotation	131
26.3	Disqualification	131
26.4	Removal	132
26.5	Dismissal as an executive director	132
26.6	Directors' rights on removal from office: compensation	132
26.7	Formalities	133
26.8	Activities prior to leaving	134
26.9	Activities after leaving	134

27 Particular companies and provisions — 135

27.1	Listed companies and their subsidiaries	135
27.2	Regulated companies	136
27.3	Companies limited by guarantee (charities)	137

Appendix A

	Standard articles of association	139

Appendix B

	Main documents required to be filed at Companies Registry.	145

Index — 149

CHAPTER 1

Points to consider before becoming a director

If you set up your own limited company you will be only too willing to become a director of it. In other cases it may be very much a matter of choice whether to become a director, though sometimes the decision will be strongly influenced by the fact that it is a promotion or for other reasons which make it difficult to refuse. In all cases, however, it is important to appreciate the obligations which are undertaken by a director of a company and what the decision involves.

Listed below are some of the main factors which should be considered before agreeing to become a director of a company. Clearly not all of these will apply in every case. Two of the most important factors are knowing the company itself and trust in the people who run the company. Other points to consider are these:

1.1 The nature of a limited company

You need to have a general understanding of what a limited company is, how it functions, and what the relationship is between the directors and the shareholders. If, in the early stages of a company, the directors are also the only shareholders, the distinction between their respective powers may seem of little practical importance, but it can be of great significance later when the company has outside shareholders or if disagreements arise. Understanding the distinction is also essential for administering the company correctly.

1.2 The responsibilities of a director

A director owes responsibilities to the company and others, and also must ensure that the company meets its statutory obligations. A failure to fulfil these responsibilities can lead to a director incurring fines or penalties, and even personal financial liability for the debts of the company or imprisonment for the worst offences. It is important therefore to understand what the responsibilities are, and the steps which should be taken to make sure you fulfil your responsibilities. Honesty on its own is not sufficient.

1.3 Independence

The personal responsibility which rests with each director means that a director has to be prepared to act independently, if necessary contrary to the views of other directors.

If you are being appointed a director to "represent" a major shareholder, parent company or other party, you have to bear in mind that your duties as a director are owed to the company (not to your appointor) and you cannot simply follow the "instructions" of your appointor.

1.4 Time

If it is your own company or if you already work full-time for the company, the time required for fulfilling the role of a director should not normally be a problem. However in other cases you should assess what is likely to be involved, how many meetings directors hold and generally how much time is likely to be needed to keep abreast of the company's affairs in order to carry out your responsibilities properly. It is important that companies hold directors' meetings on a fairly regular basis and the time of a director's appointment can be a good time at which to raise this.

1.5 Information

As will be mentioned later, directors need regular financial and other information in order to fulfil their responsibilities properly. Again, the time of your appointment is a good time to assess how the company provides this and how satisfactory it is.

1.6 Qualifications

In general, under UK company law, a director does not need to have any qualifications, nor does he need to be British or resident in Britain. Indeed all the directors could be foreign nationals residing abroad.

Sometimes the company's articles of association require directors to hold a certain number of shares in the company. If so, it is necessary to purchase the shares within two months of appointment (or sooner if so required by the articles).

Apart from a few exceptions of very limited application, the only persons who cannot be directors of a company are persons who are bankrupt or persons who have had court orders made against them disqualifying them from being directors. A person under the age of 18 can be a director (unless the articles state otherwise); so also can a limited company be a director of another company.

In the case of companies involved in certain regulated types of business (particularly banking, insurance, and financial services) it will usually be necessary for persons becoming directors of those companies to satisfy the appropriate regulatory bodies that they are fit and proper persons to hold the position of director. If a person is becoming managing director (or chief executive) of such a company, the prior approval of the relevant regulatory authority is generally necessary before the appointment can be made.

1.7 Restrictions

Because of their special position in relation to the company, there are certain kinds of transaction (eg loans or "significant property transactions") which directors cannot enter into with the company or which they can only enter into subject to restrictions or subject to shareholder approval. These restrictions often do not apply to employees of the company. These extra restrictions applying to directors need to be appreciated. In this respect a director is worse off than an employee.

1.8 Conflicts

If a director is employed by a different company from the one in which he is proposing to become a director he should also check his own contract of employment to make sure that there are no special restrictions preventing him from taking up the outside directorship.

Also, whilst there is no absolute legal prohibition on a person being a director of two directly competing companies, in practice, it would be extremely difficult properly to fulfil one's duties to both companies because of the conflict of interest which would arise and the problems of confidential information.

1.9 Memorandum and articles of association

An intending director should check the company's memorandum and articles of association (either obtaining a copy from the company itself or by carrying out a company search at the Companies Registry). Particular initial points to check would be the precise name of the company (usually clause 1 of the memorandum), the main objects clause (usually clause 3(a) of the memorandum) and to see whether there is any reference to a maximum number of directors in the articles of association (to ensure that the appointment will be within the permitted maximum number). The importance of the precise name and the objects of the company is explained later. Other important points to check in the articles are also mentioned later.

1.10 Latest audited accounts

Unless it is a new company a copy of the last available accounts of the company should be obtained so as to have a knowledge of the company's financial position. If the latest available accounts seem very old (compared with the time limits for preparing accounts referred to later) then an explanation should be sought since directors have a personal liability for ensuring that accounts are promptly prepared, and it may suggest there is some problem if accounts are in arrears.

Also, if the latest audited accounts show a very weak financial position, then a director should appreciate the extra responsibilities which fall on directors in the event of impending insolvency.

1.11 Listed companies and their subsidiaries

If you are becoming a director of a company whose shares are listed on the Stock Exchange or of a subsidiary of a listed company, then you should familiarise yourself with the additional provisions which apply to such companies. Further reference is made to this in 27.1.

1.12 Shareholders' agreement

If you are setting up a company jointly with other persons, with each of you holding shares and all or some of you acting as directors, then you should take legal advice about whether to have a shareholders' agreement so as to make sure you have adequate legal protection – otherwise majority rule will prevail and, for example, you could be voted off the board or find that dividends are not paid when you expected they would be. Special articles or a shareholders' agreement could cover these and other similar matters.

Also, if you become a director of a company in which there is an existing shareholders' agreement, then you may need to bear in mind the provisions of such an agreement if it regulates how the company is to operate.

CHAPTER 2

How a limited company operates

2.1 Distinguishing features of a limited company

It is not intended to discuss the question of whether it is better to establish a business as a limited company as opposed to an unincorporated business or partnership. However there are two principal advantages which a limited company has. First of all, a limited company is a separate legal entity, quite distinct from the shareholders who establish the company. This means that it is the company itself which owns the assets and is liable for the debts of the business. What the shareholders own is shares (which they may transfer) in the company. Even if one person owns all the shares in a company (one share being registered in the name of a nominee because in law a company must have nominally at least two shareholders) the company legally is a distinct "person" from the shareholder.

The second advantage of a limited company is that, while partners in an unincorporated business have unlimited liability for the debts of the business, the shareholders in a limited company have no liability for the debts beyond the amount which they have agreed to pay as share capital. Limited liability enables a company to obtain investors to put money into the company as share capital – few investors would be willing to invest if they had unlimited liability for a company's debts. This does not mean that a shareholder can never be liable for the debts of the company, but it does mean that (except in very limited circumstances) a shareholder who is purely an investor (and not also a director or involved in the management of the company) is not personally liable for the debts.

2.2 How a limited company is formed

It is a straightforward matter to establish a limited company. All that is required is to send to the Registrar of Companies the necessary documents together with the registration fee (currently £50) and the Registrar will issue a certificate of incorporation in about two or three weeks' time. The date of the certificate is the date on which the company officially comes into existence.

An alternative to forming a company oneself is to purchase a ready-made company from company formation agents (who form companies and supply these as ready-made companies which have never traded). This method can save time if a company is needed urgently, but the name of the company will generally need to be changed, which itself takes about two weeks.

The most important documents required to form a company are the memorandum of association and the articles of association, which together form the company's constitution. These documents must be subscribed by at least two persons who become the first shareholders.

2.3 The memorandum of association

This document sets out the parts of the constitution which are most relevant to third parties dealing with the company, namely:

The company's name
(a) No two companies can have exactly the same name, and if a company's name is too similar to the name of another company, the first company may be able to obtain a court injunction preventing the second company using that name or the Registrar of Companies may direct the second company to alter its name. It is particularly important for directors to know the precise name of the company since directors can, in certain circumstances, become personally liable on contracts or cheques which they sign on behalf of the company, if the name is incorrectly stated.

Country of registered office
(b) Companies have to state whether the registered office will be in England or in Wales or in Scotland. It is this provision which decides whether on corporate matters the company is subject to the courts of England and Wales or of Scotland.

The company's objects
(c) Because a limited company is an artificial legal entity, it can only properly carry out transactions which are permitted by its stated objects and powers. Again, it is important for a director to check these objects and powers (and in certain cases legal advice may be necessary on their interpretation) because directors can become personally liable if they carry out a transaction beyond the company's stated powers. This is known as an *ultra vires* transaction.

A typical example of a transaction which can present problems is a subsidiary company giving a guarantee or security for its parent company's liabilities.

Limited liability
  (d) A statement is included that the liability of the members (ie the shareholders) is limited (in the case of a public limited company, a statement will also be included that the company is a public limited company).

Share capital
  (e) Provision will be included stating the maximum amount of share capital which the company can issue. This is known as the authorised share capital.

With the single exception of the country of registered office (a company can of course change the particular address within the country) any of the provisions in the memorandum of association of the company can be altered. The company can change from being a private company to a public company (and *vice versa*) and can also change from limited liability to unlimited liability.

2.4 The articles of association

This document sets out how the company is to operate and be managed internally and includes particularly matters such as the rights of the shareholders, how shareholders' meetings are held, how directors are appointed, the powers of directors, how directors' meetings are to be held, and regulations about the transfer of shares.

There is a statutory form of model articles of association, known as Table A, and in practice most companies base their articles on this model form with adaptations. A summary of some of the more important provisions in Table A is contained in Appendix A. The articles of association can be altered.

The current Table A is the 1985 version. The articles of companies incorporated prior to 1985 will generally be based on the Table A which was in force at the time of their incorporation unless they have subsequently been updated. It is important to check the precise articles since there are various differences between the current Table A and previous versions. *It should be noted that references in this book to standard articles or to what the articles normally provide, describe the situation under the 1985 version of Table A (not the 1948 version or any earlier version).*

2.5 Types of limited company

Limited companies can be either private companies or public companies. Private companies must have the word "limited" (or "Ltd") at the end of their name and public companies must have as the last words in their name "public limited company" (or the abbreviation "plc") (or, in either case, the Welsh equivalent).

The essential difference between a public company and a private company is that a public company can offer its shares to the general public (eg by issuing a prospectus) whereas a private company can only obtain shareholders by private contact. However there are various other differences which are mentioned later; in particular there are several statutory provisions or restrictions which apply to public companies which do not apply to private companies since public companies are subject to greater control than private companies.

A public company must have a minimum paid up share capital of £50,000. Also, once a public company is incorporated, it can only start trading once it has obtained a trading certificate. This is obtained by confirming to the Registrar of Companies that the paid up share capital of £50,000 has been paid to the company.

Numerically, private companies are by far the largest number of companies in the UK. Although, in practice, most larger companies are public companies, there are many very substantial private companies since, if a company does not wish to issue its shares to the public, there is no reason why it should not remain a private company.

In addition there is a different category of limited companies. These are formed as companies limited by guarantee. This form of company does not have a share capital and is mainly used for charities or non-profit making organisations, not for trading companies. The members guarantee to pay a specific sum (usually £1) in the event of the company's winding-up.

2.6 Safeguards for third parties

Limited liability means ultimately that if a company goes into insolvent liquidation, creditors may not get their debts paid and will have no claim against the shareholders for their loss. In dealing with a limited company, third parties always face some degree of risk that the company may become insolvent and they may lose their money – even very well-known companies have unexpectedly hit financial difficulties. However the law contains various controls on limited companies and their directors to ensure that the privilege of limited liability is not abused. The main controls include:

Disclosure of company name
   (a) Every limited company has to state its name clearly on its notepaper, order forms and contracts so that third parties will be

aware from its name that it is a limited liability company which they are dealing with.

Filing documents at the Registry
(b) Every limited company has to file at the Companies Registry various documents and information. These are available for inspection by the public so that third parties are able to obtain financial and other information about the company. The types of documents which have to be filed include the company's memorandum and articles of association and all changes to these documents, annual accounts, details of the company's share capital, details of its directors, and particulars of mortgages created by the company.

Audit of accounts
(c) The annual accounts which every limited company has to prepare and file at the Companies Registry have first to be audited by independent accountants so that third parties can place some reliance on the figures contained in the accounts (unless the company is "dormant" and passes appropriate resolutions). Also, there are detailed statutory requirements as to what information has to be contained in the accounts.

Maintenance of share capital
(d) Third parties may place reliance on the amount of paid up share capital which a company has and so there are statutory restrictions on the manner in which a company can repay or reduce its paid up share capital.

Improper trading
(e) The privilege of limited liability is designed to protect shareholders where the business fails. It is not designed to protect those who carry on the business of a company fraudulently or recklessly or when they trade without proper regard for the rights of third parties. Statute therefore provides that directors can be made personally liable for the debts of a company if they trade improperly.

Minimum number of shareholders
(f) A company must always have at least two shareholders (one of them can be a nominee). If the number of shareholders is reduced to one for more than six months then the shareholder is personally liable for all debts of the company contracted in the period in question.

2.7 Relationship between shareholders and directors

The two bodies which can exercise power in a company are the shareholders (also called "members") and the board of directors. Their powers are prescribed by company law and by the company's articles of association. Generally speaking their powers are these:

The shareholders
(a) They have the power to alter the company's memorandum and articles of association and to approve particular transactions or re-organisations of the company (including winding-up the company) which either company law or the articles require to be approved by the shareholders. The shareholders in practice have no power to manage the business of the company themselves but under the standard articles they can pass special resolutions limiting the directors' authority or giving specific directions, and also it is they who ultimately appoint and can remove the directors. If shareholders are not happy with the management of the company, their normal remedy is to replace the directors.

The directors
(b) The articles normally delegate to the directors the full power to manage the company. The articles also normally give them the power to appoint directors to fill a vacancy or as additional directors (provided the maximum number of directors is not exceeded). Sometimes articles put limits on the powers of directors (eg as to the maximum amount they can arrange for the company to borrow) and in such a case if the directors want to exceed the limits, then they must obtain shareholders' approval at a shareholders' meeting. The powers given to the directors are given to the board of directors as a whole, but as explained below, they can delegate their powers to particular directors.

As already mentioned, where companies are set up by two or more shareholders/directors there may be a shareholders' agreement, which contains provisions as to how powers are to be exercised by the shareholders or the directors. If there is such an agreement its terms will have been purely a matter of agreement and negotiation.

CHAPTER 3

Who and what is a director

3.1 Role of a director

Stated simply a director is one of the persons appointed to direct and control the management of a company on behalf of the shareholders. However it is easier to understand how and why a director's duties arise if the role is divided into three elements:

Agent
(a) A company is an artificial entity. It is unable to do anything except by acting through individuals as its agents, such as its directors. When a director is authorised to carry out a transaction on behalf of a company, he is acting as the company's agent, and like any other agent he must ensure that he keeps within the terms of what he is authorised to do.

Controller
(b) As a member of the board of directors of a company, the director takes part in the decisions as to what the company should do. Not only therefore is he the agent of the company, but he is also one of the people who decides what action the company will take. Some of the difficulties which arise in relation to a director's duties occur when the director has a personal interest in a transaction which the company is proposing to enter into. For example, a director may own an asset which the company is intending to purchase, or the director may have a large shareholding in another company with which the company intends to do business. In all such cases, there is a potential conflict of interest and various duties apply in these situations. These duties are sometimes known as "fiduciary duties" (which also arise from his position as agent).

Employee
(c) Where a director is performing an executive role in a company, he will also be an employee of the company, and the normal rules as to the rights and duties of employees will arise. Clearly when a director is negotiating the terms and conditions of his employment a conflict of interest situation arises of the kind referred to in (b) above.

3.2 Who is a director

There is usually no difficulty in deciding who are the directors of a company. The person concerned will be described as a "director" and he will sit as a member of the board of directors. However, in particular companies, especially non-profit-making companies, the board of directors may be called some other name, eg the "council of management" or "governors", and in such a case each of the members of that body will be regarded legally as a director, even though called by a different name. The duties of a director apply to any person who performs the functions of a director.

A director may have some description attached to his name (eg "Financial Director", "Sales Director", "Managing Director") but essentially none of these descriptions affect the general duties which apply to him in his capacity as a director. The description will imply however that he has separate executive duties, and will generally reflect the executive role which he is intended to fulfil and for which he will be responsible.

Where a director has a contract of employment with the company, then he is usually described as an "Executive Director".

In some companies employees are given titles such as "Associate Director" or "Assistant Director" or "Director of XYZ Division", but without those persons intended to be members of the board of directors. Such persons are not directors in the legal sense and the use of such titles can lead to a degree of confusion and third parties may assume that such a person has the authority of a director. Furthermore, if such persons are invited from time to time to attend board meetings there is inevitably a risk that they may find themselves legally regarded as subject to the duties and responsibilities of a director. If a company is going to appoint persons with titles of this nature, it is desirable expressly to refer to such titles in the articles and make it clear they are not legally intended to be directors.

3.3 Shadow directors

By statute a person is regarded as a director even though he is not formally appointed a director, if in fact he is a person in accordance with whose directions the board of directors are accustomed to act. It is not possible therefore for someone to avoid the duties and responsibilities of a director by nominating other people as directors who will obey his instructions. A person who controls a company in this way is known as a "shadow director" and most of the duties and responsibilities of a director apply equally to him. A parent company may find that it becomes a shadow director of its subsidiary if it dictates to its subsidiary how it should act on a regular basis.

3.4 Alternate directors

The articles of a company often permit a director to appoint another person to act as a director in his place, when he is unable to do so. The articles usually provide that such an "alternate director" is responsible for his own actions and duties in the same way as any other director, so that he will, during his appointment, be subject to the duties and responsibilities of directorship. However the precise terms of the articles need to be checked in every case.

3.5 General duties of a director

There are many detailed duties which a director has and which are dealt with later, but it may be as well to summarise here the general nature of these duties:

To act honestly and in the best interests of the company
  (a) Directors must act honestly and they must promote the company's interests, not their own. Also, when exercising their powers, they must use them for the company's benefit and not for some other motive. In certain circumstances a director has also to consider the interests of the employees and additionally particularly where any possibility of insolvency may arise, they have a duty to consider the interests of creditors.

Duty of skill and care
  (b) A director must, in acting as a director, exercise the degree of skill and care which can reasonably be expected from a person of his knowledge and experience. A person who is not a business expert is not expected to show the same degree of skill as someone who, for example, a financial director who is a qualified accountant, may be expected to have a greater knowledge of accounting matters. A person who is a full-time executive director may be expected to be more aware of day to day matters within the company. In any event a director must act sensibly and reasonably within his range of knowledge and where appropriate he will need to consider taking advice. Also he must show reasonable diligence in performing his role – he cannot expect to be regarded as diligent if he fails to attend board meetings without reasonable excuse or takes no interest in the company.

   A director is not automatically liable for wrongdoings committed by other directors but he can be liable if he has in any way participated in the wrongdoing or has failed to take reasonable steps to check what was going on. Certainly if a director finds out that something wrong has occurred, then he must take active steps to ensure that it is put right.

Duty to creditors
(c) If insolvency becomes a possibility, directors have a statutory duty to creditors if it ought to be clear to the directors that there is no reasonable prospect that the company can avoid going into insolvent liquidation.

In such a case, directors must take every possible step to minimise loss to the company's creditors, otherwise they face potential personal liability to contribute to the company's assets for the benefit of creditors.

Duty not to abuse position
(d) A director must not obtain undisclosed benefits from his position, and he has a statutory duty to disclose his interest in any transaction to the board of directors.

Statutory duties and responsibilities
(e) Directors have a large number of duties and responsibilities not only under company legislation but also under many other types of legislation.

3.6 Number of directors

A private company must have at least one director, but, if only one, he cannot also act as company secretary. A public company must have at least two directors. The articles will state whether the minimum number of directors must be greater than those numbers and whether there is any maximum number of directors.

CHAPTER 4

Appointment of directors

4.1 How appointments are made

A person appointed as a director should check first of all that he has been properly appointed. The method of appointing directors is set out in the company's articles of association, but generally the following apply:
  (a) The first directors are nominated by the subscribers, ie the persons who sign the memorandum and articles of association at the time the company is incorporated, and the appointment of directors made by the subscribers is effective automatically as from incorporation.
  (b) The board of directors itself can appoint directors, provided the overall number of directors does not exceed the maximum (if any) permitted by the articles of association. Sometimes such appointment needs to be re-confirmed at the next annual general meeting.
  (c) The shareholders can appoint directors at a shareholders' meeting and can increase any maximum permitted number of directors.
  (d) Sometimes articles of association give particular classes of shareholders a right to appoint directors, and in such a case directors can be appointed by that particular class of shareholders (often merely by signing a form of appointment).
  (e) Where a company is a subsidiary company, the power to appoint directors is often given expressly to the parent company in the articles.

In every case, before a director is effectively appointed, he must sign a form, consenting to become a director of the company. This is done on the form which has to be sent to the Companies Registry notifying the appointment.

In the case of public companies special notice (28 days) has to be given to the company before a director over the age of 70 is appointed. However the articles can waive this requirement.

4.2 Checklist of steps to be taken

When a new director is appointed, there are various formal steps which need to be taken, particularly:
  (a) There should be the appropriate documentation showing the appointment (minute of board meeting or shareholders' meeting or form of appointment by class of shareholders).

(b) The director must supply to the company details of his full name, private address, nationality, occupation, date of birth (if it is a public company or its subsidiary) and particulars of other directorships which he has held in the UK during the past five years, since this information is required for various company documents. He also needs to notify the company of any shareholding which he (or certain associates) has in the company (see **12.1** below).

(c) The appointment of the director has to be notified on the appropriate form to the Companies Registry, and the director has to sign that form showing his consent to act as a director.

(d) The director's name has to be entered in the Register of Directors.

(e) It will usually be necessary to notify the company's bank of the new director, with a revised bank mandate form.

(f) If the company is listed on the Stock Exchange, or is regulated by some other regulatory body, then it will be necessary to notify the Stock Exchange and any relevant regulatory body of the appointment of the director.

(g) If a director has interests in particular companies with which the company may (or does) do business, then he should consider making a general disclosure of such interests to the board by written notice (see **10.2** and **10.3** below).

(h) If the articles of the company permit the appointment of alternate directors, then the director may consider whether to appoint an alternate director. This tends to be more important when the voting structure of the company at board meetings is delicately balanced.

4.3 Employment contract

If the director is to be an executive director, then he will want to be sure that at the time of his appointment his terms of employment are clear and agreed and have been properly approved by the board of directors. All the usual matters such as remuneration, benefits, holidays etc need to be dealt with, but perhaps the most important are the description of the precise role which the director is expected to perform and the period of notice required to terminate the employment. Provided the terms are clear it does not make any legal difference whether the contract takes the form of a letter of appointment or whether it is a more formal service contract. As mentioned in **11.3** below it is generally not possible for a company to make loans to a director so loans should not form part of the remuneration arrangements unless they come within the limited exceptions. Also, a director cannot be given a service contract of more than five years without shareholder approval – see **11.2** below.

CHAPTER 5

Directors' detailed duties – general duties

5.1 General

In accepting appointment as a director of a company, an individual assumes a wide variety of general legal duties, arising from the fact that, as explained in **3.1** above, a director's role is composed of different elements, such as agent and controller and, in the case of an executive director, also as an employee. The duties referred to in this chapter and chapter 6 are duties which the director owes to the company, and it is the company (or its liquidator, if the company is in liquidation) which can enforce the duties or claim in respect of any breach of the duties. The duties can be divided into general duties (dealt with in this chapter), and the so-called fiduciary duties which are dealt with in chapter 6.

When these detailed duties and responsibilities are set down in writing, they tend to appear somewhat daunting. However it has to be borne in mind that every agent or employee owes duties to the person who engages him. The difference in the case of a director is that being a responsible officer of a company means there are a larger number of these duties, with the addition of statutory duties which have been imposed to ensure that companies are properly operated. However provided a director is aware of the scope of his duties and appreciates that the company must be treated as a separate entity, there is no reason why, if he acts prudently, he should have any reason to fear these duties and responsibilities, though in appropriate circumstances it may be advisable for him to take legal or accounting advice to ensure that he performs his duties correctly.

5.2 Care and skill

In considering directors' duties of care and skill it is necessary to distinguish between the duties of a director as a member of the board and his duties if he is also an executive director of the company.

Duties as a member of the board

(a) The board as a whole is responsible for the management of the company. It exercises that management at board meetings. As mentioned earlier, there are generally no qualifications which a person needs to have to be a director, and the shareholders can really choose whom they like. Arising from this background, the early court cases decided that a director is not required to show any greater degree of skill than is reasonably to be expected from a person of *his actual* knowledge and experience. If the shareholders choose someone to be a director who has no knowledge of the type of business then, it has been said, they can hardly complain if his lack of experience in that type of business leads to problems. On the other hand, if a director does have experience of the type of business or has special qualifications, then he must give the company the benefit of his experience and qualifications and will be judged by the standard appropriate to his particular knowledge and experience. For example, if a director is professionally qualified or has considerable business experience then he will be judged by the standard appropriate to his qualifications or experience.

In managing the company's business, directors must exercise reasonable care, but obviously they do not guarantee profits or particular result. They are not liable for errors of judgment or because things do not turn out the way that had been hoped, provided they have, within the limits of their own particular experience and knowledge, tried to deal with matters diligently and have tried to give sensible consideration to their decisions.

On the whole, it may be said that in the past courts have not looked for a particularly high degree of skill on the part of directors in a general sense, but have tended to be stricter in relation to directors' fiduciary duties (see chapter 6). However there are three qualifications to this statement. First of all, many of the court cases are fairly old and directors, particularly in larger companies or public companies, nowadays may be expected to be somewhat more diligent than in the past. Secondly, if the director is an executive director, then the considerations in sub-paragraph (b) would apply. Thirdly, statute has imposed certain additional responsibilities in recent years particularly in relation to insolvency (see chapter 15). The trend appears to be towards expecting a higher standard of care and diligence from directors.

Duties as an executive
(b) If a director has executive responsibilities within the company and is required to devote all or a substantial part of his time to the business of the company, then he is an employee. If he is skilled or has qualifications in a particular type of work, then like any other employee he will be expected to exercise reasonable skill and competence in carrying out his work. For example, if an executive

director is in some kind of engineering company and is a qualified engineer, then he would be expected to show the skill of a reasonably competent engineer.

It is not always appreciated that every employee has a potential liability to his employer for negligence in his work. In most situations in the case of an employee, if he is negligent, it is perhaps more likely to lead to a reprimand or perhaps ultimately dismissal. However in the case of a director, particularly if it is a serious case of negligence, there is a greater possibility that the company might make some kind of claim against the director.

Even where a director has no special skills or qualifications, he would, like any other employee, still be expected to exercise reasonable care in performing his work.

5.3 Attending board meetings: time and attention

An executive director will be expected to devote the time and attention to his duties that are set out in his contract of employment, often a full-time requirement. In the case of non-executive directors, they are not obliged to devote the whole or a definite part of their time to their duties, unless there is some special agreement which requires them to do so.

A non-executive director is expected to attend board meetings if he reasonably can. He would be neglectful of his duties if he failed to make any effort to attend board meetings. In the past there have been few, if any, cases where a non-executive director has been held liable to the company in damages for failing to attend board meetings, and it was considered that the remedy lay more with the shareholders that they should remove such a director (or under the standard articles the directors themselves can remove a director if he fails to attend board meetings for more than six months). In the case of executive directors, because they are required to devote their time to the company, they would be expected to attend board meetings wherever possible.

In practice nowadays directors should make all reasonable efforts to attend board meetings, otherwise they will find it very difficult to fulfil their role and if they inadvertently participate in some incorrect action which they did not fully understand (through irregular attendance at meetings), they might well find it harder to obtain relief from the court (see chapter 7) or to avoid liability for wrongful trading (see **15.3** below). The corollary is that a person should consider very carefully before taking on a directorship if, by reason of distance or other commitments, he is very unlikely to be able to attend board meetings with any regularity.

5.4 Delegation: responsibility for acts of others

The standard articles permit directors to delegate powers to particular directors (eg a managing director) or to a committee of directors. Likewise, in practice, within the internal management of a company, particularly a large one, the implementation of board decisions and policy will be dealt with by ordinary executives of the company.

As indicated in 5.2 above a director can be liable to the company if he himself is negligent and obviously he can be liable also if he himself deliberately does wrong. However the question then arises as to whether directors can be liable if they have delegated matters to other persons (including directors) who act improperly.

The answer is that a director can be held liable for the acts of other persons within the company, but only in certain circumstances. If the board have delegated a particular function to a director, for example a managing director, and there are no suspicious circumstances and that other person acts improperly, then the general rule is that the other directors are not liable. However what the board has to bear in mind is that the shareholders have entrusted overall management to all of the directors jointly, and they must therefore exercise some degree of supervision over anyone to whom they delegate powers. Directors must question, and keep a proper control over, what is going on. They cannot simply delegate powers to a managing director (or indeed any other official in the company) and not check up at all on what is going on. There have been several cases in which a managing director has effectively been left to manage the entire business and if and when there have been board meetings, the other directors have simply approved without question what has been done. If the other directors act in that manner, then they can be personally liable for the wrongdoing of the managing director. Directors must ensure that they know what is being done and if they do not understand what the managing director or other person is doing, they must ask questions and obtain further information so that they can give proper consideration before deciding whether or not to approve what is proposed.

A director can be liable if he participates in any way in improper acts carried out by other directors. A director who attends a board meeting which approves a particular course of action which is wrong will be personally liable. It is no excuse for the director to say that he was not paying attention or did not understand what was being done, if he should have known.

However, provided directors do use reasonable efforts to exercise supervision, they should not be liable for the default of other directors or employees to whom matters have been delegated in accordance with the company's articles and internal management.

A further point is that directors must exercise reasonable care in the way they permit the business to be conducted. For example, a director can be held liable if he signs cheques at the request of another director (or official) without having any knowledge of what the cheque is for. Likewise a director could be held liable if he signed blank cheques for other employees to fill in.

5.5 Duty not to exceed powers

The articles state what powers are given to the directors, and likewise the memorandum of association sets out the powers which the company itself has. It is the duty of the directors to ensure that not only do they keep within the company's powers but also that they keep within the powers actually given to them. If directors exceed their powers then the company would be entitled to recover from them for any loss suffered by the company. The directors' liability to make good any such loss is generally an absolute liability except in one limited circumstance, namely where directors have exceeded their powers by paying a dividend when there are insufficient profits – in such a case the courts have decided that, provided the directors honestly believed, after making reasonable enquiry, that there were sufficient profits, then they are not liable. However it is a limited exception and in all other cases directors would be liable if they exceeded their powers.

5.6 Duty to have regard to the interests of employees

By statute directors are required to have regard, in the performance of their functions, not only to the interests of the shareholders, but also to the interests of the company's employees in general. However the statutory provision merely states that they must include the interests of the company's employees in their deliberations. It does not require that any particular priority be given to them or indeed that it should ultimately influence their decision. Like all the other duties referred to in this chapter (and chapter 6) it is a duty to the company, and employees cannot enforce it directly. The practical effect of this statutory duty is therefore somewhat unclear.

Under the Health and Safety at Work Act (and related legislation) employers have various general and detailed duties towards their employees and others. In particular there is a general duty for every employer to ensure, so far as is reasonably practicable, the health, safety and welfare at work of all its employees. Where a company is an employer, the directors should take steps to ensure that the company's statutory duties are performed – a director himself can be convicted of an offence if a contravention of the statute is committed by the company with the "consent or connivance" of the director, or if it is attributable to any "neglect" on the part of the director.

5.7 Duty to creditors

In general terms directors do not owe duties to creditors while the company is solvent since their duties are owed to the company itself. However in certain circumstances, particularly when insolvency is imminent, directors do have to consider the position of creditors:
  (a) Directors can be made personally liable if they conduct the business with intent to defraud creditors (see **15.2** below in respect of fraudulent trading).
  (b) Once it is clear that there is no reasonable prospect of the company avoiding going into insolvent liquidation, directors have a duty to take every step with a view to minimising the potential loss to the company's creditors (see **15.3** below in relation to wrongful trading).
  (c) Where it is clear that the company is insolvent, the directors must not favour particular creditors (see **15.6** below regarding voidable preferences) – they must treat creditors equally.
  (d) When redeeming share capital or repaying share capital or providing financial assistance for the acquisition of shares (where this is permitted) directors have to consider the position of creditors (see chapters 19 and 20).

5.8 Duty to consumers or the community

Obviously a company has to have regard to consumers in relation to the goods or services it supplies to ensure that they are of an appropriate standard and, in this respect, is subject to the general law and statute. However, generally directors have no special duties to consumers or the community at large. The directors' duty is to act in the best interests of the company but obviously improving goodwill can be in the interests of the company.

5.9 Statutory obligations

The Companies Acts impose a large number of obligations on directors. The main ones are set out in relevant sections.

Many other statutes impose obligations on companies in the operation of their business, and the general principles on which directors can be held liable for these are set out in **14.4** below.

CHAPTER 6

Directors' detailed duties—fiduciary duties

6.1 General

Arising from the director's role as agent and also someone who controls the company, a director has what are known as "fiduciary duties", ie duties which are in some sense similar to the duties which a trustee has. They are, in essence, duties of good faith, honesty and fair dealing, to take into account the fact that the director occupies a privileged position in relation to the company. These duties are described below, and it would be fair to say that generally the courts have been harsher in applying fiduciary duties to directors than they have been in applying the duties of care and skill referred to in chapter 5. It must be emphasised that directors can be liable for breach of their fiduciary duties even though they have not been guilty of any real dishonesty.

6.2 Duty to act in the best interests of the company

A private individual is, within the law, free to act in whatever way he pleases: he can give away his money or act for whatever motive he wishes. However one of the main fiduciary duties of a director is that he must act honestly and in good faith in the interests of the company as a whole. If directors reach a decision in what *they* genuinely believe to be the best interests of the company then their decision will not generally be challengeable as being in breach of their fiduciary duties even if someone else might have reached a different decision. It may, depending on the circumstances, be a breach of their duties of skill and care, but it will not be a breach of their fiduciary duties.

A few remarks can be made to clarify this duty. First of all, directors must distinguish between whether they and the company have the power to do something and whether it is in the best interests of the company as a whole actually to do it. Secondly, the fact that a transaction may also benefit the directors or some other person (eg as a shareholder) does not mean that it is not in the best interests of the company, provided the directors genuinely believe it to be so. Thirdly, the directors must consider the company and its shareholders as a whole, and in appropriate cases consider the interests of future shareholders.

The easiest way to understand the duty is to consider circumstances where directors might not be acting in the best interests of the company as a whole:

(a) If the directors are clearly acting in the interests of themselves or of some other person, but not the company. For example, if the directors sell one of the company's assets to one of themselves or some other person at what is clearly less than its value, this would not be acting in the best interests of the company.

(b) If the directors fail to consider the company's own interests at all. For example, if the company is a subsidiary in a group of companies and the directors of the subsidiary simply act on the parent company's instructions to enter into a transaction, without giving any consideration at all to the company's own interests, that would not be acting in the best interests of the subsidiary company. In law a subsidiary company is a quite distinct company and its directors must consider its own interests. Of course, in many cases in respect of transactions within a group, there will often be some overall benefit to a subsidiary company in a transaction which the parent company wishes to enter into, but the directors of the subsidiary must give proper consideration to the matter. Particular types of situation where this may arise are where the parent company wishes the subsidiary to give a guarantee for the group indebtedness or to transfer some asset within the group.

(c) If the directors agree among themselves to give each other extravagant remuneration or benefits. As indicated in **11.2** below, provided the articles so permit, directors can have service agreements with the company, but the directors must also consider the interests of the company when deciding the terms, hence the desirability, particularly in larger companies, to have at least some independent non-executive directors. An example of where entering into service contracts might not be in the best interests of the company would be if the directors deliberately did this when a takeover offer seemed imminent in order to protect their own position.

(d) If directors discriminate unfairly between shareholders. For example, if shares have been issued partly paid and directors are making a call for a further payment on the shares, then they should do so fairly, and not in a way which benefits themselves or other favoured shareholders.

(e) If a director has entered into some kind of voting agreement as to how he will exercise his discretion. It is the duty of directors to consider matters on their merits at the time and decide them in the best interests of the company – they must not fetter their discretion by agreeing with some third party in advance how they will decide the issue when it arises.

6.3 Duty not to exercise powers for a collateral purpose

As part of the directors' duty to act in the best interests of the company, it is their duty not to exercise their powers for a collateral purpose (or mainly for a collateral purpose, if there is more than one purpose). While directors are given powers by the company, they must exercise those powers for proper purposes. Again, it may be easiest to give some examples:

(a) If directors have been given power by the company to issue shares, then they must exercise that power in the interests of the company. If directors issue shares for the purpose of trying to prevent a takeover bid, then they are not exercising the powers in the interests of the company since the power to issue shares is granted to directors primarily to enable them to raise capital for the company when it is actually required.

Likewise, if directors were to issue shares to themselves for the purpose of ensuring that they could not be voted off the board.

(b) If the company's articles of association state that the directors have a discretion to refuse to register share transfers on particular grounds, then they must exercise that discretion for one of the grounds stated in the articles.

(c) Sometimes the articles of association (though this is not in the standard articles) may permit the directors to remove a director by resolution of the board. However in exercising that power they must use it in the interests of the company and not for some private purpose of the other directors (eg to remove a director who is raising legitimate questions about the conduct of other directors).

6.4 Duty not to compete

There is no definite legal prohibition on a person acting as a director of two directly competing companies. However the duties of confidentiality and acting in the best interests of a company would in practice make it very difficult indeed for a director properly to sit on the board of two directly competing companies. For example, as a director, an individual will be aware of a company's plans for the future, and it is difficult to see how the director could then sit on the board of a competitor company and discuss their plans for the future.

If the director is an executive director then it is probably more clear-cut that he cannot be a director of a competing company, either because his service contract expressly prohibits this or alternatively because there will usually be an implied obligation not to do so.

6.5 Duty of confidentiality

A director will, in the course of his duties, be aware of confidential information relating to the company, its customers and its business. A director must not disclose or make use of that confidential information for any purpose otherwise than for the benefit of the company.

6.6 Duty to disclose interests

As mentioned in chapter 10, a director has a statutory duty to disclose any personal interest which he has in relation to any business or transaction being carried on or proposed to be carried on by the company.

6.7 Duty not to make secret profits

As part of a director's fiduciary duties, he must not make secret profits out of his position. For example, if a director receives information of a potential business opportunity in his capacity as a director of the company, he must not use that opportunity for his own purposes. If he does so, then he will be in breach of his fiduciary duties to the company (since it is the company's information which he has used) and he will be accountable to the company for any profit which he makes. It does not appear to make any difference that the company itself may not have been in a position to take up the opportunity. Also, if the director has obtained the information in this way, he cannot avoid his obligations to the company by resigning and then personally taking up the opportunity.

In essence, if a business opportunity comes to the company it belongs to the company. If the company is able to make use of the opportunity then the directors must ensure that it does. If the company is not able to take up the opportunity then if the articles permit directors to do so, the director may be able to take up this opportunity personally provided he declares his interest, otherwise it would be necessary to obtain specific shareholder approval to do so.

6.8 Duty not to misapply company assets

Whilst the directors do not have legal ownership of the company's assets, they do have effective control of them, and they must use them and employ them for the proper purposes of the company, and in the best interests of the company.

For example, they must not use company funds to pay their own personal debts, or in any other way misuse or misapply company assets for purposes which are not permitted, otherwise they are in breach of their duties.

6.9 Nominee directors

A nominee director, who is appointed to represent the interests of a particular shareholder or group of shareholders, should also be careful to avoid any conflict of interest. It is perfectly lawful – and not uncommon practice – to act as a nominee director, but on no account should the director accept any obligation towards his appointor to act or vote in accordance with the appointor's directions; he must be left free to exercise his own judgment as to what will serve the interests of the company best and he must not put the interests of his appointor above those of the company itself. If the director is expected to undertake a reporting function, advising his appointor in detail of the company's affairs, he should ensure that he has the company's approval of such arrangement and the disclosure of relevant information to the appointor, since a shareholder does not, in the absence of agreement, have any special right of access to information other than under the limited general publicity requirements of the Companies Act. His main role should be to present the views of the party he represents at board level, but he should retain substantial discretion of his own as to how he exercises his powers at the end of the day and should not place the interests of his appointor above those of the company.

CHAPTER 7

Relief from liability

7.1 General

The duties referred to in chapters 5 and 6 are duties owed to the company, and a director is liable to the company if he breaches those duties. The question that arises is whether, if a director has been in breach of his duties, inadvertently or otherwise, he can be relieved of liability.

7.2 Relief from liability by court

By statute the court has a discretion in certain circumstances to relieve a director, wholly or partly, from his liability to the company for negligence, default, breach of duty or breach of trust. However this is only available if the court is satisfied that the director has acted honestly and reasonably and that having regard to all the circumstances of the case (including those connected with his appointment) he ought fairly to be excused. It must be noted that the provision only applies to a director's liability to the company or for infringement of the Companies Acts – it does *not* apply to any liability which a director may have to third parties (eg under a personal guarantee to a creditor of the company). Also, it does not apply to liability for wrongful trading (see **15.3** below) since a director's liability for wrongful trading depends on the particular factors stated, and there is no extra scope for the court's discretion.

In order to bring himself within this statutory relief, a director needs to show that all three conditions are satisfied (honesty, reasonableness and appropriate circumstances). So far as acting reasonably is concerned, the director must show that he has acted in a manner in which "a man of affairs with reasonable care and circumspection could reasonably be expected to act". For example, the conditions may be satisfied where the director has considered the matter carefully and endeavoured to act in accordance with legal advice. On the other hand, a director may not be regarded as having acted reasonably if, in a complex situation, he has failed to take any advice or has failed to give full consideration to the matter.

Honesty is not, on its own, sufficient to obtain relief from the court. However where a director has acted honestly and also endeavoured to act prudently and sensibly, then a director may be able to obtain relief from the court.

7.3 Exemption from liability in articles or by contract

In view of directors' potential liabilities to the company it might be tempting to insert in the company's articles of association (or perhaps in the director's service contract with the company) a general exclusion clause exempting a director in advance from all liability to the company for breaches of his duties. However statute makes any such provision ineffective, and so such a general exclusion clause is not possible.

However, the statutory restriction on such exclusion clauses does not appear to apply to a provision in the articles which relaxes the rules about directors having a conflict of interest with the company. The articles can therefore permit directors to deal freely with the company without restriction and without having to account for personal profits to the company provided the director has properly disclosed his interest to the board (see **10.2** below).

Although articles cannot exempt a director in advance from his liabilities to the company, it is permissible for the articles to state that the company will compensate a director for any costs which he incurs where the court ultimately decides that the director is not liable to the company or where the court exempts the director from liability in accordance with 7.2 above.

7.4 Settlement of claim

Although it is not possible to indemnify a director in advance for breach of his duties, there appears to be no reason in principle why a company should not enter into a binding settlement with a director (or former director) after a breach of duty has come to light. However, the other directors in coming to such a settlement would have to make sure that the settlement was made in good faith and in the interests of the company.

7.5 Ratification

Where directors have committed some breach of their duty or something has been done incorrectly or there is some technical irregularity, it is in most cases possible for the shareholders to ratify the matter by an ordinary resolution at a shareholders' meeting. It is essential that in the circular to shareholders with the notice of meeting the position is set out clearly so that shareholders appreciate that they are being asked to ratify an irregularity or breach of duties.

There are, however, certain transactions which a majority of shareholders cannot ratify, namely transactions which are totally beyond the powers of the company altogether or those which infringe the personal rights of a shareholder or those which constitute a fraud on the minority of shareholders (see 22.7 below).

If, however, all the shareholders are unanimous in their wish to ratify a transaction, then such a ratification would probably be effective in relation to all matters that were properly within the objects and powers of the company. However such a ratification would not be effective if the company was insolvent or the position was such that creditors would be prejudiced by any such ratification.

7.6 Insurance

It is possible for directors to obtain insurance for their liabilities as a director. Such insurance would not, of course, cover a director for his own dishonesty or any intentional breaches of his duties, nor for any special contractual liabilities undertaken by the director personally, eg warranties given by the director personally on a share issue or under a share purchase agreement or guarantees (for example of leases) given by directors personally. There are also likely to be various other specific exclusions depending on the precise policy wording.

Where directors give personal warranties on share issues or share purchase agreements or the like, it can be possible to obtain separate specific insurance relating to such liabilities.

The Companies Act 1989 will permit companies themselves to pay for directors to have insurance against liability for breach of their duties.

CHAPTER 8

Directors' meetings

8.1 The need for meetings

As explained in chapter 9, the articles of a company usually provide that all the powers of managing the company are entrusted to the board of directors. This means that the board as a whole is given the power to manage, not directors individually, and the articles will then go on to provide how the board is to meet to reach its decisions. It is generally speaking, therefore, by way of meetings that the board makes its decisions.

If the articles permit there to be only one director in the company, and the company only has one director, then no "meeting" is necessary since the sole director will decide everything himself. Also, articles generally permit the board to delegate particular powers to a managing director or some other director or directors. If the particular powers are delegated to a director, then those powers can be exercised by the director concerned and no meeting is necessary, unless the delegation is to two or more directors.

8.2 Written resolutions

Articles generally permit the board to reach decisions by a written resolution signed by all the directors, instead of a meeting, with each director signing either the form of resolution or a duplicate copy of it (so that all the copies together constitute signature by all the directors). Normally the articles provide that written resolutions must be signed by all the directors, but in principle there is no reason why the articles should not provide that a written resolution is to be regarded as passed if a certain majority of the directors sign it.

While written resolutions are satisfactory for formal matters or for confirming decisions which have already been discussed, they are not usually a particularly satisfactory way of reaching decisions on matters which would benefit from a discussion among the directors. In such cases a meeting would be preferable since this allows further information to be provided and for points to be aired and the background to the decision to be given. The chairman or managing director might be able to obtain the signatures of all directors to a particular resolution, which seems very sensible on the face of it, but if the matter were discussed at a meeting, it may well be that other points would arise which would make some other course of action desirable.

Written resolutions may seem a quick and simple way of obtaining decisions on non-controversial matters but in practice, particularly if the signatures of all directors are required by the articles, it can sometimes take longer to achieve this than if a board meeting is called.

8.3 Frequency of meetings

Articles generally leave it entirely up to the directors as to when they hold their meetings. It is desirable that directors should hold meetings so that matters can be properly discussed and up to date financial and other information regarding the company assessed. There is often great merit in most companies having board meetings at regular intervals. In appropriate cases particular or routine matters can be delegated to a committee.

One cannot generalise about how often directors' meetings should be held. A non-executive director, or a director of a company with a large board whose own duties are limited to a restricted aspect of the company's business, will usually want to have regular and frequent meetings to make sure he can keep an overall view of the company's affairs and activities. On the other hand, in a small company with only two or three directors who work together and all know exactly what is going on, formal meetings may be necessary less frequently.

Apart from normal business matters and the approval of business contracts, the following are examples of some common matters which require board decisions:

(a) appointing one of the directors as chairman;
(b) appointing an additional director, or appointing a managing director or setting up a committee of the board;
(c) approving service contracts for directors or appointing a company secretary;
(d) issuing shares or approving share transfers;
(e) convening the annual general meeting and extraordinary general meetings and approving circulars and notices of meetings;
(f) approving the use of the company seal (eg to execute deeds, mortgages, share certificates);
(g) approving annual accounts and recommending dividends;
(h) changing the registered office;
(i) completing a bank mandate for the company's bank account;
(j) appointing the first auditors or filling a vacancy in auditors.

8.4 General conduct of board meetings

The articles generally leave it to the directors as to how meetings are conducted. The standard articles state that any director may summon a meeting and that the secretary shall summon a meeting at the request of any director.

8.5 Notice of meetings

Notice of meetings must be given to all directors even if they are unlikely to attend. However, articles generally state that notice need not be given to a director who is abroad; if however he has appointed an alternate director under the articles, the alternate will normally be entitled to notice. Reasonable notice has to be given of the meeting, but the notice does not need to be in writing and, unless the articles state otherwise, need not say what the business to be transacted is. In practice it is obviously desirable (and common) that a notice would state the agenda for the meeting since there will often be papers and matters to be considered in advance. The articles could, if desired, state more precisely how meetings were to be called and what notice was required, and likewise the board itself from time to time may make decisions as to how meetings are to be conducted.

Where directors are known at the time of their appointment to be resident abroad (eg in the case of a subsidiary of an overseas parent company) it may be appropriate that the articles should expressly provide that overseas directors are entitled to notice of meetings.

There is no definitive answer as to what constitutes reasonable notice of a meeting. It depends on the circumstances. If all the directors work in the same building and are actually there at the time, very brief notice may be sufficient. Otherwise the notice should be such as to give the directors a reasonable opportunity to be present. It has to be appreciated that a directors' meeting is not in the same category as a shareholders' meeting and that directors are persons who have a duty to attend to the company's affairs and are generally paid to do so. If, when a director is given notice of a meeting, he feels it is simply too short then he should clearly state this at the time, otherwise he may subsequently be regarded as having waived any right to object to the shortness of the notice.

8.6 Quorum

As regards the quorum for a meeting, the standard articles state that the quorum shall be fixed by the directors, and unless so fixed, is two directors. Often, particularly in larger companies, the quorum will be set at a higher figure so that one is sure of a reasonably representative decision. On the other hand one does not want too high a quorum since there may at times be difficulty in achieving it.

8.7 Difficulty obtaining a quorum

It may on occasion be necessary to hold a meeting, but difficult to gather together a quorum of directors and impossible to gather all necessary signatures for a written resolution; or, directors may want their views to be expressed at a meeting which they cannot personally attend. There are two possible ways of getting around this:

Alternate directors
(a) Often, the articles permit a director to appoint someone else to take his place, a so-called "alternate director", who will be a kind of proxy with power to perform all the functions of the director appointing him but with more extensive duties than a simple proxy since normally the articles provide that an alternate director "shall be deemed for all purposes to be a director and shall alone be responsible for his own acts and defaults". An appointment as alternate director is, therefore, not to be undertaken lightly.

An appointment (or removal) of an alternate is normally required to be made in writing by notice given to the company. The appointment may be general and for an indefinite period, or limited to attendance at a particular meeting or to a particular exercise of the appointing director's powers.

Meetings by conference telephone
(b) Occasionally, the articles expressly permit board meetings to be conducted by means of a conference telephone call – usually with precise rules about how the meeting is to be conducted in such circumstances.

Unless there is an express article permitting board "meetings" to be held by phone, it does not appear legally permissible to have a meeting by phone (though obviously if a meeting had been duly convened and there is a quorum present, other directors can participate by phone).

8.8 Chairman

The standard articles provide that the board may appoint a chairman, and may remove him from office. While in office, the chairman presides at every board meeting, but if he is unwilling to act or is not present within five minutes of the time of the meeting, then the directors may appoint another of their number to act.

8.9 Decisions

Unless the articles otherwise state, decisions of the board are taken by a simple majority vote on all matters, and the standard articles give the chairman a casting vote in the event of an equality of votes. The standard articles provide that an alternate director can vote and if the alternate director is also a director in his own right, then he may also exercise his own vote as well.

8.10 Voting where director has an interest

The standard articles state that a director is not entitled to vote or be counted in the quorum on any matter in which he has, directly or indirectly, an interest or duty which is material and which conflicts with the interests of the company unless it relates to:
(a) giving him a guarantee, security or indemnity in respect of money lent to, or an obligation incurred for the benefit of, the company or any of its subsidiaries;
(b) the giving to a third party of a guarantee, security or indemnity in respect of an obligation of the company or its subsidiaries for which a director has assumed responsibility;
(c) his subscribing or agreeing to subscribe for any shares, debentures or other securities of the company or any of its subsidiaries;
(d) a retirement benefit scheme which is subject to Inland Revenue approval.

Under the standard articles the company may by ordinary resolution relax these provisions. In practice, the articles of many companies, particularly private companies, often provide that the director *may* vote and be counted in the quorum in respect of any matter in which he has an interest, provided the director has disclosed his interest. This is obviously a point on which the articles need to be checked carefully.

8.11 Minutes of meetings

The board is required to keep minutes of its meetings. It is not necessary for minutes to be detailed, and it is generally sufficient if they show the decisions which have been made – for example "IT WAS RESOLVED that the company should enter into an agreement with X Limited on the terms of a draft produced to the meeting and initialled for identification by the chairman". The minutes should state which directors were present at the meeting.

All appointments of officers of the company (and managing directors and chairman) should be minuted, in addition to all other decisions.

Whilst it is generally sufficient to record in minutes simply the decisions which are reached, there are some particular points which it may be desirable to refer to on particular occasions when somewhat fuller minutes than normal may be appropriate. For example:
- (a) Directors have a duty to declare their interest in transactions. To avoid any doubt that this was done, it is desirable to record this in the minutes, where this applies. When a director does have an interest, other directors have to take extra care that the transaction is in the best interests of the company and evidence in the minutes that the other directors properly considered this may be desirable. Also, it is desirable to show there was a clear majority in favour without the "interested" director's vote.
- (b) Where a crucial decision has been taken, particularly one where directors have special duties, it can be desirable to make the minutes more detailed to show that the directors did take into account relevant matters. For example, if the company's financial position is serious and the board is meeting to decide whether to carry on trading, detailed minutes would be appropriate to show that the directors considered relevant professional advice and the company's up to date financial position and if they decided to carry on trading, why they felt this was appropriate. It may also be sensible to show the length of time the meeting lasted.
- (c) Also, if it is not on the face of it apparent that it is in the company's interests to enter into a particular transaction, it would be desirable to record the background and the way in which the directors felt the company's interests would be furthered or exactly what was the benefit to the company.
- (d) If the directors are sending an important circular to their shareholders or are approving a prospectus, detailed minutes showing that the directors went through the documents carefully are helpful.
- (e) Also, as mentioned elsewhere (see, for example, **19.3** and **20.3** below), in various circumstances directors have to make statutory declarations before certain kinds of transactions are dealt with – in these cases again it would be useful for more detailed minutes to be made showing that the matter was carefully considered by the board.

As in the case of shareholders' meetings, minutes of directors' meetings, if signed by the chairman of the meeting or the next meeting, are evidence of the proceedings and until the contrary is proved, the meeting is deemed to have been duly held.

8.12 Circulation of minutes

There is no statutory requirement to circulate to the directors minutes of their meetings or of committees of the directors. However, it is useful and desirable to do so, particularly so that the directors who have not been present at meetings can know what is going on and in the case of committees of the board, so that the board as a whole knows what the committee is doing.

8.13 Committees and delegation

Articles generally provide that the board can delegate any of their powers to (i) committees consisting of one or more directors or (ii) any managing director or (iii) any director holding executive office. In delegating its powers, the board can impose restrictions and limitations on the exercise of the powers delegated and it may revoke the powers at any time. A resolution appointing a committee need not name the particular directors, but could state simply that any two or three directors are to be a committee for the purpose.

There are clear advantages in the board being able to delegate in this manner. Particularly in very large companies it would be impossible for every decision to be made by the board as a whole. The power to give particular directors decision-making authority over certain matters is very useful. However it is important that the board resolution which makes the delegation should set out clearly what the precise powers are and any limits which apply. This not only protects the company but it also protects the director concerned.

A committee of the board may be used in many circumstances. A particular situation would be where the board has agreed "in principle" on a certain course of action but the details have to be approved, in which case a committee could be set up to approve the details on behalf of the board. If a director has a conflicting interest in a matter, a committee could be used to consider the matter, obviously excluding the "interested" director. However the power of establishing committees should not be used generally for the purpose of excluding a particular director from management decisions.

Where a committee of two or more directors is set up the board may set out how the committee is to hold its meetings but in the absence of any such directions, then the articles which apply to board meetings would apply also to committee meetings.

8.14 Dissent

Board decisions are generally made by majority vote. If a director is out-voted by his fellow directors on any issue, then that is just the usual consequence of majority rule. However a situation may arise where the disagreement is on a serious matter where the director feels that more is at stake than simply majority rule.

If the decision is one of general policy (with no other overtones) then the director may feel sufficiently strongly about the matter that he wishes to resign. There is no reason why he should not do so and he may also wish that his reasons for resigning should be recorded in writing.

Situations may however arise where the matter is not one simply of policy but which the director feels affects his duties as a director. For example, the majority might decide on a course of action which the director considers improper or illegal or the director may not be happy with the way matters are being handled. Alternatively, the company's financial position may be serious and the majority may nonetheless feel that they should carry on trading whereas the minority director feels that the company is insolvent and there is no prospect of recovering the position. What should a minority director do in such a situation?

The point which has to be appreciated in these situations is that a director's duties are wide and his over-riding duty is to the company, its shareholders, creditors and employees. The director would probably be considered to be failing in his over-riding duties if in such a situation he were to do nothing other than simply resign or walk away from the situation or no longer attend board meetings. One cannot generalise as to what a director should do in such a situation but some of the possible courses of action would be these. First of all the director could consider putting his views forward in writing and circulating all the other directors. Secondly he could consider taking legal advice, on whether there was any action which he could or should take to prevent what was proposed by the majority. Certainly he should not simply resign as a director until he has considered the situation very carefully. In view of his over-riding duties, resigning as a director in such a situation may not of itself terminate his responsibility for anything that might happen. For example, once it is clear that there is no reasonable prospect of the company avoiding insolvent liquidation each director must take every step to minimise loss to the company's creditors (see **15.7** below). Also, if some of the directors are not acting properly, the other directors may be the only people who can control the situation.

CHAPTER 9

Directors' powers

9.1 Power of the board generally

As has been mentioned, almost invariably the management of the company's business is delegated to the board of directors by the articles of association. Indeed this is the main division of functions between the shareholders and the directors: the shareholders have the power to alter the framework of the constitution of the company and to appoint the directors, and it is the directors who manage the business. The standard articles have the following provision:

> "Subject to the provisions of the [Companies Act], the memorandum and the articles and to any directions given by special resolution, the business of the company shall be managed by the directors who may exercise all the powers of the company. No alteration of the memorandum or articles and no such direction shall invalidate any prior act of the directors which would have been valid if that alteration had not been made or that direction had not been given. The powers given by this regulation shall not be limited by any special power given to the directors by the articles and a meeting of directors at which a quorum is present may exercise all powers exercisable by the directors."

It is important to appreciate that it is the directors as a whole who, acting together, are given these powers. The manner in which the directors exercise the powers granted to them is by passing board resolutions, generally at board meetings.

As will be seen from the terms of the standard articles no alteration of the articles and no direction is to invalidate any prior act of the directors.

9.2 Limitation of directors' powers

The directors derive their powers from the articles, and therefore it is essential for directors to check the precise wording of their articles to see whether there are any particular restrictions or limitations on their powers. The kind of restrictions which are sometimes inserted are restrictions which limit the borrowing powers of the directors perhaps to a certain multiplier of the paid up share capital or some other formula – if so directors must keep within those limits or alternatively obtain the approval of their shareholders to exceed the limits.

In addition to restrictions which are contained in the articles themselves, it will be noted that under the standard articles shareholders are given the right to make directions by special resolution which may impose restrictions on the powers of the directors. The shareholders can of course also alter the articles by special resolution.

In addition to these limitations, there are various statutory requirements which prevent directors exercising certain powers or carrying out certain transactions, unless shareholders have authorised or approved such matters. These particularly relate to the directors' powers to issue shares (see **18.4** below) and particular transactions in which directors are personally interested (see chapter 11).

9.3 Board exceeding their own powers or the powers of the company

If a transaction exceeds the powers of the board or the company then the transaction may not be valid and may therefore not be binding. In considering the validity of any transaction it is important to distinguish between (i) whether the company's own powers have been exceeded or (ii) whether (even though the transaction is within the company's own powers) the directors have exceeded the powers given to them.

Exceeding powers of company
(a) The objects and powers of a company are set out in its memorandum of association and a company must keep its activities within the objects and powers expressly stated. If the company acts outside its objects or powers, then the transaction is technically described as *ultra vires* (ie beyond the powers of the company). The general rule has been that any such transactions would be ineffective and would not be binding on the company. However certain statutory protection is now given to third parties (see **9.5** below), and as a result such transactions will now in most cases be binding upon the company. However the directors can still be liable to the company if they enter into transactions beyond the company's powers. Also if for some reason the statutory protection does not apply (and so the transaction is not binding) they could be liable to third parties if they misrepresented to the third party that the company had power to carry out such a transaction.

Board (as a whole) exceeding its powers
(b) Generally the board is given wide powers of management under the articles, but as indicated, these powers may (under the standard articles) be restricted by special resolutions or indeed the

articles of a particular company may limit the powers given to the directors in some way (eg in relation to the extent of borrowing).

If the board as a whole exceeded its powers, the question as to whether the transaction was binding on the company has depended upon certain limited statutory protection given to third parties and presumptions they could make about a company's internal procedures, but if neither of these applied the transaction was not binding. However under the Companies Act 1989 there will be much greater legal protection in favour of third parties, which will apply in most cases (see **9.5** below). However the board will still be liable to the company if it exceeds its actual powers.

9.4 Power of an individual director

There is a general legal principle that where powers are delegated to a person, that person is not entitled to delegate them further unless he is expressly authorised to do so. The power of managing the company's business is delegated to the board of directors, and therefore they can only delegate those powers to an individual director or directors if they are expressly authorised to do so under the articles (but again the new statutory protection in favour of third parties, in **9.5** below, will now usually apply if the board delegates powers without being entitled to do so). The standard articles authorise the board to delegate any of its powers either to a committee (consisting of one or more directors) or to any managing director or other executive director. However, as always, it is wise to check the articles.

Express authority
(a) If the board of directors duly delegates powers to an individual director then clearly that director is authorised to enter into transactions within the scope of the express powers delegated to him, and those transactions will be fully binding on the company.

No express authority
(b) However frequently the precise powers which are delegated to a particular director are not spelled out in detail. For example, a director may have been appointed "managing director" or "sales director" without any express statement of his powers. Indeed, looking further down a company's structure, one may find persons appointed as "manager" or "branch manager", and again it may not be expressly stated what authority such a person is intended to have. In such cases the individual concerned is impliedly authorised to do all such things as fall within the usual scope of the position to which he has been appointed (but subject always to any

express limitations which may be imposed). In such cases transactions effected by such an individual within the scope of such implied authority will be binding upon the company.

Effect of exceeding authority
(c) If an individual exceeds the authority given to him by the company then there are three potential consequences. First of all, the transaction may not be binding on the company – the statutory protection in favour of third parties (see **9.5** below) does not appear to give protection to third parties in relation to the lack of authority of an individual director (as opposed to the board as a whole) except in the limited case where the board had no authority to delegate (but did so).

Secondly, any individual who enters into a transaction on behalf of a company, impliedly represents that he has the necessary authority to commit the company and therefore if the transaction is not binding, the individual can be liable to that third party for breach of his representation.

Thirdly, if the transaction is binding on the company, then the individual may be liable to the company for exceeding his authority, though the board or the shareholders (if the board does not have the necessary power) may ratify the transaction.

If a director is in any doubt as to whether he has the necessary authority to enter into any transaction (or take any action) then he should obtain clear authority. Also, any third party dealing with an individual director should obtain clear evidence of his authority if there is any doubt.

9.5 Statutory protection given to third parties dealing with a company

Third parties who deal with a limited company often do not check the company's memorandum and articles nor require specific proof of directors' authority, and in the past there has been some limited statutory protection given to third parties dealing with a company in good faith. This protection has previously been qualified and subject to restrictions with the result that in several cases the protection has not been effective. However the Companies Act 1989 will be introducing wider statutory protection in favour of third parties as set out below. However it should be emphasised that the statutory protection does not give protection to third parties in every case.

Company's objects (the ultra vires rule)
(a) So far as third parties are concerned, they are not bound to enquire

into the objects of a company and transactions will now be binding even though they may go beyond the stated objects of the company. However this protection does not affect the rights of any member of the company to take proceedings to prevent the company entering into a transaction outside its objects (assuming the member is aware of the transaction before it is entered into) nor does it affect the directors' liability to the company for exceeding the company's objects. Directors must therefore still make sure that they keep within the objects of the company, or they may be personally liable.

The Companies Act 1989 will enable companies in the future to state their objects in much wider terms than before. A company can now state its objects as being to act as a general commercial company, the effect of which is that the company can carry on any trade or business whatsoever and that the company has power to do all such things as are incidental or conducive to the carrying on of any trade or business by it.

The powers of directors
(b) The 1989 Act also provides that in favour of a person dealing with a company in good faith, the power of the board of directors to bind the company, or authorise others to do so, is deemed to be free of any limitation under the company's memorandum and articles. It is also provided that a party to a transaction with a company is not bound to enquire about the objects of the company or any limitation on the power of the board of directors, and indeed a person is not to be regarded as acting in bad faith by reason only of the fact that he is aware the transaction is beyond the power of the directors.

Some particular points to note in respect of the statutory protection are these:
  (i)   where the limitation on the directors' powers arises from the fact that the transaction is not permitted by the company's objects, then the company can ratify the transaction by special resolution (if it would not otherwise be binding);
  (ii) the statutory protection does not affect the right of a member of the company to bring proceedings to restrain (in advance) any proposed transaction which is beyond the power of the directors;
  (iii) it does not affect the liability of the directors to the company for exceeding their powers;
  (iv) the statutory protection does not apply to protect a director of the company (or its holding company) or any person

(v) connected with such a director (or a company associated with such a director) where such persons are involved in the transaction;
(v) the statutory protection would not apply where the third party is acting in bad faith, eg where there is fraud involved.

Whilst greater statutory protection is now given to third parties, and as a result transactions may be binding on the company, nonetheless it is still essential that directors should check carefully what the objects of the company are and what the powers of the directors are and to keep within those objects and powers. Otherwise directors may still find themselves liable to the company for exceeding their authority.

9.6 Misuse of directors' powers

Even where a particular act or transaction is within the capacity of the company and even if the directors are properly authorised to enter into that transaction on the company's behalf, it may nevertheless amount to a misuse by the directors of the powers they have. The directors have a duty to the company not to exercise their powers for a collateral purpose – see **6.3** above.

9.7 Gratuitous transactions

Directors may wish their company to make gifts or donations, for example to charities or political parties. This gives rise to considerations of whether it is within the scope of the company's objects or powers, and also (having regard to the general duties of directors towards their companies) whether such a gift or donation would be *bona fide* in the interests of the company itself.

Often the objects clause of the company will include a provision expressly providing for the making of donations for charitable, benevolent or public purposes. It has been said that "the objects of a company need not be commercial; they can be charitable or philanthropic; indeed, they can be whatever the original incorporators wish, provided that they are legal. Nor is there any reason why a company should not part with its funds gratuitously or for non-commercial reasons if to do so is within its declared objects". So, it is necessary to interpret what the memorandum says to see whether the contemplated gift is one of the company's objects. Even so, caution should be exercised if the company is, or is in danger of becoming, insolvent, or if the "gift" is to be made to a shareholder since that may amount to an unlawful distribution or return of capital to the shareholder.

If there is no express object or power in the memorandum, there may nevertheless be an implied power if this is reasonably incidental to the attainment of the company's other objects. If so, and there is a benefit to the company, the transaction may be valid. In the case of political donations, say, it is commonly thought that it may be in the interests of the company to advance the policies of the political party in question. Also, the statutory protection to third parties in **9.5** above could apply if there is no authority in a company's memorandum and articles of association to make gifts.

If the company becomes insolvent, however, there is a power for the liquidator or administrator to apply to the court in respect of transactions entered into by the company at an "undervalue". A transaction at an undervalue includes gifts and donations, and also transactions whereby the value of the benefit received by the company is "significantly less" than the value of the performance given by the company itself. See **15.6(a)** below.

9.8 Dividends

The payment of dividends is regulated in detail by the Companies Acts, and advice should always be sought from the company's auditors as to whether a payment is permissible.

Under the Acts, distributions, whether of cash dividends or other assets, may only be made out of "profits available for the purpose", which means the company's accumulated, realised profits (so far as not previously used) less its accumulated, realised losses (so far as not previously written off in a reduction or reorganisation of capital). Public companies are further restricted, in that they may make a distribution only if, before and after the distribution, net assets are not less than the amount of called up share capital plus undistributable reserves. These questions will normally be determined by reference to the company's last annual audited accounts.

Assuming a distribution is permitted, the question of who actually has authority to declare a dividend does not depend on the Act, but principally on the articles. Normally two stages are necessary: first, the directors must decide to recommend the payment of a dividend and secondly the shareholders must declare a dividend by passing an ordinary resolution. If the directors do not recommend a dividend then one cannot be declared by the shareholders, and no dividend can exceed what the directors recommend.

As regards interim dividends, however, the directors themselves will normally have a right to pay interim dividends without reference to the shareholders, but only if it appears to them that payment is justified by the profits of the company available for distribution. Such a decision must be reached in good faith. In particular, if insufficient profits are available by reference to the last audited accounts, then formal interim accounts need to be prepared in accordance with the requirements of the Companies Act.

The directors can also pay fixed interest dividends on shares if they consider the profits justify them, and they cannot generally pay interim dividends on ordinary shares if any preferential dividend is in arrear.

Under the general law, directors can be held personally liable if they authorise a dividend to be improperly paid.

Special provisions apply to insurance companies.

9.9 Borrowing and charges

In order to borrow money, a company must have the necessary power under its memorandum of association. Normally this will be expressly provided in the "objects clause", but even if it is not it may be implied if it is reasonably incidental to the company's objects – which will almost certainly be the case for a trading company, up to a reasonable amount. If the directors cause their company to borrow money in the unlikely case where it does not have power to do so then they may be liable either to the company or to the lender in line with the principles described above. Also by statute it is a criminal offence for a public company to exercise its borrowing powers unless it has the minimum £50,000 worth of paid up share capital (which is required in order to begin trading) and has been issued with a certificate to that effect by the Registrar of Companies.

Assuming that a company has the power to borrow it will usually also have, incidental to its borrowing power, a power to give security over its assets in respect of any borrowings; however, almost invariably there will also be a separate express power to do this in the "objects clause".

If the company does grant security over its assets, the mortgage or charge or debenture must be registered at the Companies' Registry within 21 days. A director will himself be liable if he is in default in doing so, along with the company. The charge itself will still bind the company if it is not registered in time, but the lender will not be protected if the company becomes insolvent (because a liquidator will not be bound by it) or if a third party acquires an interest in the property for value.

9.10 Bank accounts and cheques

When a company opens a bank account, the bank will require a written mandate confirming the authority of individual directors (or others) to operate the accounts. For this purpose, the bank will require formal board resolutions to be passed (in the bank's standard form), and a certificate to the effect that those resolutions have been passed will have to be given to the bank.

It is important for directors to ensure that the name of the company itself is fully and accurately stated on all the company's cheques – otherwise, a director signing (or even authorising signature of) the cheques may by statute be held personally liable on the cheque.

CHAPTER 10

Directors' disclosure of interests

10.1 General

Because of directors' fiduciary duties towards the company, the general rule is that a director must not enter into any contract or arrangement with the company or have any personal interest in any transaction or arrangement in which the company is involved. This is to prevent the director being in a situation where his personal interests conflict with those of the company. However this rule would prevent a director having any employment contract with the company. It would prevent a director selling any asset to the company (even though the company was formed by the director to transfer his business into it). It would prevent a person from becoming a director of a company if his own employing company had any dealings with the company. The rule could therefore impose restrictions on what would otherwise be perfectly legitimate arrangements.

It is usual therefore for a company's articles to relax the general rule so as to permit directors to have interests in transactions in which the company is also involved and to permit the director to retain any benefits which he derives from such transactions (otherwise he would be accountable to the company).

For example, the standard articles do permit a director to have interests in contracts or arrangements in which the company is involved and to retain all benefits subject to two requirements:

(a) first of all, the director must disclose the nature and extent of any material interest he has to the board of directors;
(b) secondly, if the director does have an interest then he is not entitled to vote at the relevant meeting of the directors or committee of the directors on any such matter (nor is he allowed to be counted in the quorum for the meeting) except in four particular cases listed in **8.10** above.

However it is important for a director to check the particular articles of association of the company to see exactly what the requirements are. In the case of small private companies, the articles may permit the director to vote and be counted in the quorum for any matter in which he is interested.

10.2 Disclosure of interests

As indicated, if a director has any interest in a contract or arrangement involving the company, then he must declare his interest. Even apart from any provision in the articles, this is a statutory requirement (and it is an offence if it is not complied with).

The director is obliged to declare the nature of his interest at a meeting of the directors (a meeting of a committee of the directors is not sufficient). In the case of a proposed contract, the declaration must be made at the meeting of the directors at which the question of entering into the contract is first taken into consideration or, if the director was not at that time interested in the proposed contract, at the next meeting of the directors held after he became interested. If the director becomes interested in the contract after it is made, then the declaration must be made at the first meeting of the directors held after he became interested.

It is not necessary that the notice should be a written notice, but in practice it would be a sensible precaution either to put the declaration in the form of a written notice or alternatively to ensure that the declaration is fully and properly minuted in the minutes of the relevant directors' meeting.

10.3 General interests

A director can comply with the statutory provision (and also the provision in the standard articles regarding disclosure of interests) if he makes the declaration in respect of each particular transaction. However it is also permissible for the director to give a general notice to the company to the effect that the director is a member of a specified company or firm and is to be regarded as interested in any contract which may, after the date of the notice, be made with that company or firm or that he is to be regarded as interested in any contract which may, after the date of the notice, be made with a specified person who is connected with him.

10.4 Nature of interests which need to be disclosed

A director's duty is to disclose any direct or indirect interest in a contract or proposed contract (or transaction or arrangement) with the company. Accordingly if the director has any interest he must disclose not merely that he has an interest but also details of that interest so that the other directors will be fully aware of the position.

The question of what is exactly meant by an "interest" is an important one, but there is no clear answer. A director should therefore declare any possible interest.

10.5 Effect of disclosure of interest

Even if the articles permit directors to be interested in arrangements in which the company is involved (subject to the director first declaring his interest), it is nonetheless the duty of the directors to act in the best interests of the company. Merely because the articles may permit directors to be interested in contracts with the company does not mean that it is appropriate for a particular transaction to be entered into. The directors must give proper consideration to the matter.

10.6 Ratification by shareholders

If the articles of a company do not permit directors to enter into a particular transaction in which they are interested, then it would be necessary for the relevant director to disclose his interest to a meeting of shareholders and seek the shareholders' approval to the proposed transaction.

Likewise, if a director was interested in a contract but failed to disclose his interest properly before the contract was entered into with the company, then he could seek shareholder ratification of the transaction and his interest in it.

However, in either case, shareholder approval or ratification would not be effective if it amounted to a fraud on the minority (see 22.7 below) and the director had secured approval by exercising his own votes in favour of ratification or approval.

CHAPTER 11

Arrangements between directors and the company which are subject to restriction

11.1 General

As mentioned in chapter 10 the articles of a company generally relax the rules about directors' interests in transactions and arrangements so that directors can have an interest in contracts or arrangements in which the company is involved, provided they have disclosed their interest properly at a board meeting.

Even though directors may be interested in their company's transactions, they must still act in the best interests of the company, and if they fail to do so, then they can be held to account by the company for breach of their fiduciary duties.

However, as a result of a number of abuses, statute has intervened to provide that, even though the articles of a company may permit directors to enter into transactions freely with a company, certain transactions between a director and a company are either prohibited altogether or are subject to prior shareholder approval. The transactions in question are dealt with below.

11.2 Service contracts

General
(a) Under the standard articles the board may appoint any director to hold any executive office in the company on such terms as to remuneration or otherwise as it thinks fit (though subject always to their general duty to act in the best interests of the company). The director concerned must first disclose his interest formally (see **10.2** above), even though of course, in the case of service contracts, his interest will be obvious.

The standard articles do not permit a director to vote or be counted in the quorum regarding any resolution by which the terms of his service contract are approved, but in the case of many companies (particularly smaller private companies) the director concerned may well be permitted by the articles to be counted in the quorum and to vote even on his own terms of service.

There are no real statutory restrictions on the level of remuneration or benefits which the board may agree to pay to an executive director – though his remuneration must not be tax free (see **13.7** below). However, as already indicated, the directors must consider the best interests of the company in determining the remuneration and benefits.

Service contracts over five years
(b) One particular area of potential abuse is that the directors might grant themselves very long service contracts with the company (eg 10 years or 15 years) which would make it difficult or expensive for the company to terminate their engagement. As a result, statute now provides that if a director's service contract cannot be terminated by the company within five years, then before such a contract is entered into, it must be approved by the shareholders in general meeting. This provision applies not only to service contracts as such but also to contracts for services (eg as a self-employed consultant to the company).

Shareholder approval is not required to all the terms of the contract, but merely the length of the contract. In order for the shareholders' resolution to be effective, the proposed contract or a written memorandum setting out the full terms must be available for inspection by shareholders at the company's registered office for not less than 15 days prior to the meeting and at the meeting itself.

If a service contract or contract for services with a director is entered into by the board for more than five years without shareholder approval then the term relating to the length of the contract is void and the agreement is deemed to be subject to termination by the company on reasonable notice.

In order to avoid directors being able to get round the provision by a series of service contracts, the statute also provides that if, more than six months before the expiration of the period for which the original contract is to run, the company enters into a further agreement under which the director is to be employed, then the unexpired term of the original contract must be aggregated with the further contract in deciding whether the agreement exceeds five years.

Inspection of service contracts
(c) Although shareholder approval of shorter term contracts is not necessary, any contract which does not expire or cannot be terminated by the company without paying compensation within 12 months (or if there is no written contract, then a written

memorandum of its terms) must be kept available for inspection by shareholders either at the registered office or at the principal place of business (provided this is in the same country in the United Kingdom as the company's registered office) or the place where the register of members is kept. This obligation includes employment contracts with subsidiary companies as well, but there are more relaxed restrictions regarding the contracts of directors who work abroad.

Disclosure in accounts
(d) The other main requirement of publicity regarding directors' service contracts is the requirement that certain details must be published annually in the accounts. Although the directors concerned and their individual remunerations are not identified separately, the remuneration of the chairman and the highest paid director has to be stated exactly and the remuneration of other directors is required to be specified according to the number of directors earning remuneration within £5,000 bands.

11.3 Loans to directors

General prohibition on loans
(a) As a result of a number of abuses that came to light in the 1970's, statutory provisions were introduced which, broadly speaking, prohibit a company from making a loan to any of its directors subject only to certain fairly limited exceptions. The rules are fairly complex and detailed, and unless a loan falls very clearly within one of the exceptions, directors would be well advised to take expert advice. If a transaction is entered into in breach of the statutory provisions then not only is it voidable by the company but a director who authorises or permits the company to enter into any such transaction having reasonable cause to believe the company was contravening the provision, is guilty of an offence.

The statute provides that a company shall not make a loan to a director of the company or of its holding company nor shall it enter into any guarantee or provide any security in connection with a loan made to a director. It is therefore not possible to get round the prohibition on loans by arranging for a third party to make the loan to the director with the company then guaranteeing the loan to the third party. As indicated, there are certain exceptions to the prohibition and these are referred to below. Also, in the case of public companies and subsidiaries of public companies (or a company which has a public company in its group) the prohibitions are widened to include so-called quasi-loans and credit transactions as referred to below.

It should be noted that if these provisions are breached the directors who authorise the loan can be held to account personally as well as the director who actually benefits.

General exceptions
(b) There are the following exceptions to the general principle that loans to a director are prohibited:
  (i) Loans of small amounts are unrestricted, provided the aggregate amount of all such loans to that director is not more than £2,500 (to be increased to £5,000 by the Companies Act 1989).
  (ii) A company may make a loan to a director to provide him with funds to meet expenditure incurred or to be incurred by him for the purposes of the company or for the purpose of enabling him properly to perform his duties as a director. However these exceptions are subject to two provisions:
    (1) If it is done, it must be done with the prior approval of the company in general meeting (at which the purpose of expenditure, the amount of funds and the extent of the company's liability must be properly disclosed) or it must be done on condition that if approval of the company is not given at or before the next annual general meeting, the loan is to be repaid or any other liability arising under any such transaction discharged within six months.
    (2) The aggregate amount committed by a company in respect of this exception must not exceed £10,000 at any time.
  (iii) Companies whose ordinary business includes making loans or giving guarantees for loans may make loans or give guarantees for a director provided this is done in the ordinary course of its business and provided the amount and terms of the loan or guarantee are not more favourable than would have been offered to an independent third party of the same financial standing.

Additional restrictions applying to public companies (or companies in a group which includes a public company)
(c) The following additional restrictions apply to public companies or companies which are in a group which include a public company. These additional restrictions are designed to catch transactions which have a similar type of effect as a loan to a director:

(i) The above companies are prohibited from making "quasi-loans" to directors. Quasi-loans are given a fairly wide definition. Basically what the expression covers is situations where the company makes a payment to a third party on behalf of the director so that the director becomes bound to reimburse the company, for example, if the director wishes to purchase something for his personal use and arranges for the company to send a cheque in settlement of the amount due, the intention being that the director will then reimburse the company.

(ii) Making loans or quasi-loans to anyone who is "connected" with a director. "Connected" person includes the director's spouse, child, partner, associated company or trustee of a family settlement.

(iii) Giving any guarantee or security to a third party who makes a loan or quasi-loan to a director or a connected person.

(iv) Entering into a credit transaction with a director or a connected person (or providing security for a third party to enter into a credit transaction), except in certain limited circumstances. A credit transaction means an agreement for the sale of goods or land or the supply of services or the hire or lease of goods or land on deferred payment terms.

(v) Loans permitted under (b) (iii) above are limited to £50,000 (to be increased by the Companies Act 1989 to £100,000) unless the lender is a recognised bank.

It can be seen therefore that public companies (or private companies in a group which include a public company) are subject to much greater restrictions than private companies. A private company may be able to find ways of making funds available for the benefit of a director without infringing the prohibition on straightforward loans since it may be possible for the arrangements to be re-structured. However again, it is the directors' duty in relation to any such transaction to act in the best interests of the company.

Even if a loan or other transaction is permitted under the statutory provisions, details are required to be disclosed of the transactions in the annual accounts of the company.

11.4 Substantial property transactions

General prohibition
(a) Even though the articles of a company may permit directors freely to enter into transactions with the company, statute requires that "substantial property transactions" involving a director or any

person connected with a director, must first be approved by the shareholders in general meeting, otherwise the transaction is voidable by the company. Also, if approval has not been obtained from the shareholders, the director concerned or the person connected with him who is in contravention of the provision and any other director of the company who authorised the transaction are liable to account to the company for any gain which has been made directly or indirectly by the person out of the arrangement and to indemnify the company for any loss or damage resulting.

A substantial property transaction is subject to these provisions if a director of the company (or of the company's holding company) or any person connected with such a director is to acquire from or sell to the company any asset having a value in excess of (i) £50,000 or (ii) 10% of the company's net asset value, whichever is the less. The net asset value of a company for this purpose is the value of its net assets by reference to its last audited accounts or, where no accounts have been previously prepared, the amount of the company's called up share capital.

As in the case of quasi-loans, a person is connected with a director (broadly speaking) if the person is the director's spouse, child, partner, associated company or trustee of a family settlement.

Exceptions
(b) The following transactions are excluded from the statutory restrictions:
  (i) If the value of the asset in question is less than £1,000 (regardless of the company's net asset value) or if the value of the asset is less than £50,000 or 10% of the company's net asset value as above.
  (ii) Where the transaction is between companies in the same group provided all the group subsidiaries are wholly-owned.

11.5 Compensation for loss of office

There are three statutory provisions which can apply to payments made to a director by way of compensation for loss of office or in connection with his retirement from office. They do *not* apply to any payment made in good faith either by way of damages for breach of contract or by way of pension in respect of past services. In other words, the provisions will not apply where a director's service contract is terminated prematurely by the company so that he has a legal claim against the company for breach of contract, provided the compensation is paid in good faith as damages for the wrongful termination; nor will the provisions apply to a pension paid in good faith in respect of the director's past services. However, the damages or pension arrangements must be reasonable. If it desired to pay an extra large pension or to make some extra payment beyond the normal level of legal damages, then the arrangements will be subject to the following provisions:

Compensation for loss of office
  (a) It is not lawful for a company to pay to a director any compensation for loss of office or any sum in connection with his retirement from office without particulars of the proposed payment (including its amount) being disclosed to shareholders and approved by them by ordinary resolution.

Compensation in connection with approval of transfer of property
  (b) It is not lawful, in connection with the transfer of any part of the undertaking or property of a company, for any payment to be made to a director, either by the company or by anyone else, as compensation for loss of office or in connection with retirement from office unless particulars of the proposed payment (including its amount) have been disclosed to shareholders and approved by them by ordinary resolution.

Duty of disclosure in connection with takeover
  (c) Where an offer is being made for the shares in a company (or part of them) it is the duty of the director concerned to take all reasonable steps to ensure that details of any payment proposed to be made to him as compensation for loss of office or in connection with his retirement from office (including its amount) are included in or sent with any notice of offer made to shareholders. If the director fails to take the necessary steps then he is liable to a fine.

Compensation would include anything of value given to the director in the above circumstances, and where any shares are being sold by the director, any higher price obtained by him as compared with other shareholders would be regarded as compensation. If appropriate approval is not obtained, then any monies received by the director are held in trust for the company or (if paragraph (c) is not complied with) in trust for those who have sold their shares as a result of the offer in question.

CHAPTER 12

Directors' share interests and dealings

12.1 Notification of share interests in the company

A person who becomes a director of a company, and who has an interest at that time in the shares or debentures of the company, is under a statutory duty to notify the company in writing within five days after his appointment of his interest, together with details of the number of shares and debentures of each class concerned. (Saturdays, Sundays and bank holidays are disregarded in calculating the time limit.)

A director is also under a statutory duty to notify the company in writing within five days (as above) of any event as a consequence of which he becomes or ceases to be interested in shares or debentures of the company or contracts to sell any shares or debentures or obtains the right to subscribe for shares or debentures in the company.

The above provisions apply not only to shares or debentures in the company of which the person is a director, but also to those of the company's subsidiary or holding company or a fellow subsidiary company.

There are detailed and complex provisions which apply to determine when a director is to be regarded as having an "interest" in shares. Obviously if the director himself owns the shares, then he has an interest, but the statutory requirements are expressly extended to cover interests in shares held by the director's spouse or children under the age of 18. However a director is not regarded as having an interest if he holds shares merely as a trustee or nominee, with no beneficial interest at all.

12.2 Dealing in share options

It is an offence for a director to buy "put" options or "call" options (or combined options) relating to shares or debentures of his own company or any company within the same group which are listed on a stock exchange either in Great Britain or abroad. The prohibition also extends to such dealings by a director's spouse and children under age 18.

The prohibition applies to buying options; it does not apply to the director being granted an option by the company direct (eg under an executive share option scheme).

12.3 Insider dealing

General provisions
(a) Insider dealing is a criminal offence. It does not by any means apply only to directors, but it applies to any person who is or has been connected with a company and who as a result has obtained "unpublished price sensitive information". It is not possible to cover all aspects of insider dealing in this section, but the following is a general outline.

The statutory provisions apply where an individual is, or at any time in the preceding six months has been, connected with a company (including as a director of that company or another group company).

Under the statutory provisions, such a person is prohibited both from dealing in the securities of his company (or other group companies) on a recognised stock exchange or (in respect of publicly marketed shares) through an off-market dealer and from dealing in the shares of other companies with which his company is doing business (or contemplating doing business), if in either case:
(i) he has information as a result of holding office as a director (or any other connection) and he knows it to be "unpublished price sensitive information"; and
(ii) it would be reasonable to expect such a person not to disclose that information except for the proper performance of his functions.

Not only do the provisions prohibit a person with price-sensitive information dealing in a company's shares, but they also prohibit such a person from counselling or procuring any other person to do so, and generally prohibit the passing on of the information to a third party if there is reasonable cause to believe the third party would deal or use the information improperly.

"Unpublished price sensitive information"
(b) "Unpublished price sensitive information" is information concerning specific matters relating to or of concern to that company (ie not information of a general nature) and which is not generally known to those accustomed or likely to deal in those securities but which would be likely to affect the price materially if they were to know of it.

Principal application
(c) The prohibitions will be of concern principally to the directors of companies whose securities are listed on a recognised stock exchange or are publicly marketed, or to directors of other

companies within the same group, but not to most directors of private companies. However directors of private companies should be aware that they can be directly affected if their own company is involved in an important transaction with a company whose shares are traded on a recognised stock exchange or publicly marketed.

Stock Exchange Model Code
(d) The Stock Exchange Model Code for directors of listed companies gives guidance in respect of share dealings by directors, to take into account the fact that directors will always be in possession of more information than can at any particular time be published. The code requires that a director should not deal in any of the securities of the company at any time when he is in possession of unpublished price sensitive information not only regarding his own company but also when, by virtue of his position as a director of his own company, he is in possession of unpublished price sensitive information relating to another listed company. Subject to that it is suggested that a director should not deal in any securities of his own company without first notifying the chairman (or other director appointed for the purpose) and that during the period of two months immediately preceding the preliminary announcement of the company's annual or half-yearly results, a director should generally not deal in the securities of his company at all.

CHAPTER 13

Directors' remuneration, pension and other benefits

13.1 General considerations

The question of directors' remuneration and benefits is governed by a number of general principles. First of all, unless the articles otherwise permit, the directors would not be entitled to obtain remuneration or other benefits from the company because of their fiduciary relationship with the company. However, in practice, articles do permit directors to receive remuneration, but it is wise to check the company's articles to see if there are any unusual provisions. The usual article will state that the amount of directors' remuneration is to be determined by an ordinary resolution of the shareholders and, unless otherwise stated, is to accrue from day to day (so that if a director ceased to be a director in the middle of a year he would be entitled to a proportion of the remuneration for that year). The articles also normally state that the directors may appoint any one of their number to any executive position in the company on such terms – including as to remuneration – as they think fit.

Effectively what all this means is that remuneration purely for holding the office of director (ie with no executive responsibilities) is determined by the shareholders, whereas the remuneration and other benefits for any executive role which a director has, is decided upon by the directors themselves.

There are three over-riding restrictions in relation to directors' remuneration. First of all, when directors are deciding the amount to pay one of their number for executive duties, they must act in good faith in the best interests of the company. Secondly, there are certain statutory restrictions on what benefits directors may receive. And finally, a director will normally be prohibited from voting on (or counting towards the quorum for) his own remuneration as an executive – and even if the articles do permit him to vote he should generally refrain from doing so and ensure there is a completely "independent" majority of directors approving.

13.2 Directors' fees and expenses

The term "directors' fees" is the term generally used to describe the remuneration for the non-executive role of being a director. The amount of the directors' fees is generally a routine item on the agenda for the annual general meeting. In the case of executive directors, their service agreements will generally state whether such directors' fees are to be paid in addition to their executive salary or are to be treated as being included in their executive salary – likewise any directors' fees which may be payable to them as directors of subsidiary companies.

The standard articles also state that the directors may be paid all travelling, hotel and other expenses properly incurred by them in connection with attending board and shareholders' meetings or otherwise in connection with the discharge of their duties. Directors therefore can (under the standard articles) resolve to pay such expenses to themselves, if they so wish.

13.3 Remuneration as executives

Standard articles state that the board may appoint any one of their number to hold executive office on such terms as they think fit. So far as an executive director is concerned, he should check to make sure that a proper board resolution has been passed in respect of his remuneration and terms of service, ie that the resolution is in the minute book, that there was a quorum present and that his interest had been duly disclosed. In larger companies, it is quite common for non-executive directors to play a significant role in determining the remuneration to be paid to the executive directors.

The amount of remuneration to be paid to executive directors is very much a matter for the board, and if the articles are in the standard form, shareholders and creditors would not generally be entitled to question the amount. However, as always, directors have a duty to act in the best interests of the company. If the directors are the sole shareholders of the company, then the payment of most of the profits of the company (after making proper allowance for creditors) to the directors each year as directors' remuneration would generally be permissible. If, however, there are outside shareholders and the directors were paying excessively large remuneration to themselves, then the outside shareholders may be able to apply to the court on the grounds that the company is being conducted in a manner which is unfairly prejudicial to them. Equally, payment of large remuneration to a director who was doing virtually nothing for the company could well be objectionable and it could amount to misfeasance on the part of directors (as could payments to directors' spouses who take no part in the company). Likewise it could be misfeasance if the directors pay themselves excessive remuneration when the company is in financial difficulties.

13.4 Pensions

Pensions are an important part of remuneration and executive directors will normally expect to have a pension arrangement from the company. However before any such arrangements are entered into, it is necessary to check that the articles give to the directors the power to enter into pension schemes for directors. The standard articles do give the directors this power.

Pensions are a highly technical and complex subject these days, and directors need expert advice before implementing any scheme. However the following comments are intended to give a simplified bird's eye view.

Revenue approval
(a) Pension arrangements enjoy many tax benefits. Income and gains of pension funds are tax free. Also, pension contributions paid by a company on behalf of the director are not treated as benefits in kind and a director's own pension contributions enjoy tax relief. However in order to obtain these benefits, the pension scheme must be approved by the Inland Revenue.

Contracting-out
(b) A company pension scheme can be "contracted-out" of the state earnings related pension scheme.

Type of scheme/benefits
(c) For the purposes of Revenue approval, the Revenue set certain upper limits to pension benefits, and in order to obtain approval of the scheme, the benefits must be within those limits. Very broadly speaking pension schemes can provide pensions for executive directors of 1/60th of their final salary for each year of service, up to a pension of 2/3rds of the director's final salary, and a widow's pension of 4/9ths of the director's final salary. Likewise, there can be a death in service cover of four times the director's salary. There is, in addition, an uplifted scale which enables a director to obtain a full 2/3rds pension provided he has completed at least 10 years' service, but subject to bringing into account other benefits which he may have on previous pension schemes. Until 1989 there was no overall maximum pension which could be approved, but under the Finance Act 1989, in relation to pension schemes in future approval will only be available in respect of final salary up to £60,000 pa (this figure to be index linked).

On retirement, the director can commute part of his pension for a tax free cash lump sum. The amount of this cannot exceed $1\frac{1}{2}$

times final salary – the precise amount which can be taken as a lump sum being dependent upon length of service, the maximum only being available if 40 years (or in certain cases, 20 years) service has been completed.

In the case of directors who hold, with their associates, 20% of the share capital of a company there are certain restrictions which apply.

Types of scheme
(d) There are two basic alternatives. The first is a final salary scheme in which what is promised to the director is a pension of (say) 1/60th of his final salary for each year of service – in this arrangement the director may be asked to make a contribution from his own salary to the scheme, with the company being required to pay whatever is necessary to meet the balance of the cost of the benefit.

Because the director's final salary is undetermined, the cost of this arrangement is unknown, and contributions will be made by the company on actuarial estimates. The advantage of this arrangement to the director is that the director is likely to know the scale of benefit which he will obtain on retirement. The other alternative is a money purchase type scheme under which (say) the company contributes a certain percentage of the director's salary each year and the director simply obtains whatever benefits are achieved from such a contribution. The advantage from the company's point of view of this arrangement is that the cost to it of the scheme is readily ascertainable.

Unfunded arrangements
(e) Sometimes, particularly in private companies, one or more of the directors may reach close to retirement age and then realise that no adequate pension arrangements have been made for him. It is possible at that stage to set up a pension scheme and take account of the years of service he has completed up until that time. However it may require a fairly substantial capital sum to purchase the pension covering the past years and the company may not have these funds readily available – also, although there is no overall maximum which a company can pay by way of pension contribution (one of the advantages of a company pension scheme), the tax relief on a very large pension contribution may be required by the Revenue to be spread over a number of years.

In these circumstances the company and the director may consider an unfunded pension scheme, ie the company itself agrees to pay a pension without contributing to a fund. Two points arise generally on unfunded arrangements. First of all, even an unfunded arrangement has to be approved by the Revenue in order to avoid adverse tax consequences. Secondly, directors need to consider very carefully their duties generally to the company – is the proposed arrangement properly in the interests of the company; also, have the directors taken into account the overall cost of what the company is being committed to, which can be substantial.

13.5 Other benefits and expenses

Apart from the length of service agreements (see **11.2** above), loans to directors (see **11.3** above) and significant property transactions (see **11.4** above), directors can as part of their terms of employment with the company enjoy any benefits which other employees can enjoy, for example a car, or permanent health and medical schemes and the like.

So far as expenses are concerned, directors should only be entitled to receive expenses which are properly incurred in connection with the company's business. From time to time, cases come to light of companies paying for expenses of directors' spouses, gardeners at their private homes or similar. These are not expenses properly payable by the company.

13.6 Share schemes

There are currently three types of Inland Revenue approved share schemes for employees (including directors). These are:
(a) approved profit sharing schemes;
(b) approved savings related share option schemes; and
(c) approved selective share option schemes.

Approved profit sharing schemes and approved savings related share option schemes are schemes which must be available to all employees (if they are introduced) and there are comparatively low financial limits on the benefits which may be obtained under such schemes. For example, in relation to approved profit sharing schemes the annual value of shares allocated to an employee must not exceed £1,250 or 10% of his salary, but not exceeding £5,000 per annum.

In comparison, approved selective share option schemes offer potentially greater benefits and also the employees and directors who are to benefit can be selected. In order to be eligible for such a scheme a director must be a full-time director (at least working 25 hours per week). However a participant must not, together with his associates, hold more than 10% of the ordinary share capital of the company concerned. Provided the employee or director is eligible, he can be granted options over shares up to the value (at the time of grant) of £100,000 or four times his emoluments for the current (or previous) year, whichever is the higher figure. In order to obtain the tax benefits any option must be exercisable not less than three nor more than 10 years after the date of grant. The advantages of such a scheme are that the director is enabled to acquire shares in the company at the option price at the date of grant without income tax implications, and any tax liability will only arise for capital gains tax at the date of disposal of the shares.

If an approved share scheme is not possible then an unapproved incentive arrangement may be worth considering since higher rate income tax is currently the same rate as capital gains tax.

13.7 Taxation

Statute prohibits a company from paying a director remuneration free of income tax or otherwise calculated by reference to, or varying with, his or normal rates of income tax. If any such arrangement is entered into, it is deemed to be an agreement to pay gross and subject to income tax the actual sum mentioned. A director of a company is subject to PAYE and to tax, exactly the same as an employee of the company, in respect of all remuneration payable to him. In addition, a form has to be completed in respect of each director stating the benefits and expenses received by him in each year.

CHAPTER 14

Directors' liabilities to third parties

14.1 General position

A director owes various duties to the company. As explained in chapters 5–7, if a director falls short in carrying out these duties then the company (or its liquidator if it is in liquidation) can take action against the director for breach of duty or misfeasance.

This chapter relates to the liability of directors to persons other than the company. Sometimes it is assumed that because a company has limited liability, a director cannot be directly liable to third parties. Whilst this is generally true in relation to contracts, this is certainly not correct in relation to other liabilities. In practice where a company is solvent, the third party will be more likely to take action against the company rather than the director. Obviously, however, different considerations arise if the company appears to have few assets.

It is important, therefore, for a director to appreciate the circumstances in which, when acting for the company, he may be personally liable.

14.2 Contracts

General rule
(a) A director is the agent of the company. When a director enters into a contract on behalf of the company, then the general rule is that it is the company (and the company alone) which is liable on that contract. However a director must always make it absolutely clear that he is acting on the company's behalf. In any written contract he should ensure that the full and correct name of the company is clearly stated on the letter or other document which contains the contract or order and that he signs "for and on behalf of XYZ Limited". Likewise, if he is placing an order or contract by phone, he should make sure that the other person understands that it is the company contracting. If it is unclear that the director is contracting on behalf of the company, then like in any other agency situation, the director may find himself personally liable to the other party.

Liability in "tort"
(b) In recent years it has been decided that where a party has a

contractual claim for negligence he may also, in appropriate cases, claim it as a tort (ie a wrongful act giving rise to legal liability separate from any contractual relationship) (see **14.3** below). The question arises whether a director can be personally liable on a company contract in this way. If the director was not personally involved in dealing with the contract then he cannot be liable. If however the director was personally involved in carrying out the contract then there are certain circumstances in which the director can become personally liable to the third party if his actions amount to a personal "tort" by him (eg a misrepresentation or breach of a personal duty of care to the third party).

Authority of director to enter into contract
(c) If the director does not have the necessary authority from the company to enter into a particular contract on its behalf, the position is as follows. The contract may nonetheless be binding on the company (because of the protections given to third parties dealing with a company in good faith (see **9.5** above)) or because the director had apparent authority, but the director may find himself liable to the company for exceeding his own authority. Alternatively, if the third party finds that the contract is not binding on the company (because of the director's lack of authority) then the director will be personally liable to the third party because by signing on behalf of the company he impliedly warrants that he has the necessary authority to do so. Before committing the company to any contract the director should consider therefore whether the contract is within his authority. For example, somtimes when managing directors or other executives are appointed, the resolution or service contract appointing them imposes certain upper limits on their authority, otherwise the matter is to be referred back to the board.

Special situations
(d) A director can also be personally liable on a contract if he enters into the contract in the company's name before the company is actually incorporated or, in the case of a public company, before the company has obtained its trading certificate to commence business – this is issued once the minimum paid up share capital of £50,000 minimum has been received. Another example is if he acts while he is subject to a court order disqualifying him from acting as a company director (or if he is acting on the instructions of someone else who he knows is subject to such a court order). Additionally, liability may arise in certain circumstances if a director purports to enter into a contract which is outside the

company's powers (*ultra vires*) if he misrepresents the position (see chapter 9 above).

14.3 Negligence and other "torts"

Meaning

(a) The expression "torts" refers to various civil (as opposed to criminal) wrongs which do not depend on a contractual relationship between the parties, but where the law gives a third party the right to make a claim if he suffers loss or damage. Examples of "torts" are negligence (including negligent or fraudulent misstatements) where it is clear a third party may be affected, defamation, infringement of copyright and patents, nuisance etc. Where there is a contractual relationship, the same circumstances may in certain situations give rise to a separate claim in tort, independent of the contractual liability.

General rule

(b) Where an employee is acting in the course of his employment by a company and commits a "tort" then the general rule is that the company itself is "vicariously liable" to the third party for the tort, but the employee may also be held liable because the fact that he is acting on someone else's behalf does not excuse him from his personal duties to third parties. In the same way, if it is a director who himself commits the tort, then he can be personally liable to the third party.

Directors procuring "tort"

(c) However directors are not mere employees so that not only are they themselves carrying out actions on behalf of the company, but they will also be controlling the policy and running of the company. The further question that arises therefore is whether directors can be personally liable (in addition to the company) where an employee commits a tort. The general rule is that directors are not normally liable in such circumstances, but they can sometimes have such liability. The test is whether the directors themselves procured or directed or authorised the committing of the tort. If the directors in fact knew nothing about the matter then they would not be liable and it would only be the employee (or particular director concerned) who actually committed the tort who might potentially be liable to a third party in addition to the company. For other directors to be liable, it is not usually necessary that they should have realised that what was being done was a tort, nor that they should have been reckless about this. It is sufficient if they actually directed or authorised the act in question. The precise degree of involvement depends on the particular circumstances of the case, and it is unclear whether simply voting for a course of action at a director's meeting (without appreciating it was a tort) would be sufficient.

In the normal course of events, where the company has assets or insurance available to meet any such claims, then the third party would usually sue the company. However the risk for a director is higher if the company does not have assets or insurance to meet any such claim.

14.4 Criminal offences

This section deals with offences committed by a company, excluding offences under the Companies Acts which are dealt with in section 14.5 below. Almost all offences are capable of being committed by a company – eg fraud, theft, etc – except for crimes where a truly "personal" element is essential. The question is whether a director can be personally liable for offences committed by the company. The matter is of some importance since nowadays there are so many statutes which create offences, some of which are serious, while others are of a fairly technical nature. Some criminal offences are of "strict" liability (ie it is not necessary to prove any intention to commit the crime on the part of the person concerned for there to be an offence) but in other cases a greater or lesser degree of intention or negligence is necessary before there is an offence.

Offences requiring intention

(a) If an offence requires a criminal intent, then an individual director will only be liable if he himself actively and intentionally participated in the criminal offence, ie that he himself had the necessary intention, or in those cases where a degree of negligence or recklessness is required, that he himself had the necessary degree of recklessness or negligence.

Strict liability

(b) If the statute which creates the offence makes it an offence of strict liability (ie it is irrelevant whether or not there has been any intention or negligence or recklessness) and no mention is made in the statute of directors being liable, then generally speaking if the company has committed an offence of that nature, the company alone will be liable for it. However statutes often make express provision for directors to be liable also if they personally have been guilty of neglect or have connived at the offence (the wording depending upon the precise statute).

14.5 Companies Act offences

The Companies Acts create a huge number of statutory offences for failing to comply with the statutory requirements. Many of these are mentioned specifically in other sections – for example, failing to file documents with the Registrar of Companies when required, purchasing or giving financial assistance for the purchase of a company's shares except as permitted, offences in relation to the issue of prospectuses, and so on. Usually the penalty is a fine (sometimes on a day by day basis), but sometimes the penalty is more severe.

For most offences where the company is in default of statutory requirements the Companies Acts specify that any director who is himself "in defáult" – which means if he knowingly and wilfully (ie deliberately and intentionally) authorises or permits the default in question – is also guilty of an offence, and if so he will also be liable for the penalty.

In addition, there are specific offences under the Companies Acts applying to directors, the most important of which are noted under relevant chapter headings.

14.6 Liability for tax

Directors are not in general liable for corporate taxes, but by way of exception, directors can still be made liable personally for betting and bingo duty if the company fails to pay.

Under certain tax legislation however (eg national insurance contributions and Customs & Excise duties), non-payment of the amount due by the company is an offence, and directors can also be guilty of the offence if it is shown that the failure was committed with their consent, or connivance or by their neglect. They are not however liable for the tax itself.

14.7 Guarantees

Particularly in the case of small private companies, directors are often requested personally to provide guarantees to third parties, eg landlords in respect of leases or banks in respect of overdrafts, loans or other liabilities. A director should consider very carefully before giving such a guarantee, and legal advice should be taken. Sometimes in the case of small companies with small share capitals, it is difficult ultimately to avoid providing a guarantee in the early days of the company's existence. However, if at all possible, the effect of giving the guarantee should be mitigated by including provisions for directors to terminate their liability on notice (for example if they cease to be directors) or imposing some upper limits on liability or some circumstance or event (eg when the overdraft is reduced to a certain figure) at which time the guarantee will cease to apply.

In the case of guarantees of leases, it should be borne in mind that the original lessee of premises (and the guarantor) are liable throughout the term of the lease, even if the premises are vacated and the lease sold to a third party. A guarantee of a lease can therefore be a very onerous obligation, unless limitations can be negotiated.

14.8 Bills of exchange

If a director signs a bill of exchange (eg a cheque) on which the correct name of the company is not properly stated, then the director is, by statute, personally liable on that bill of exchange.

14.9 Other liabilities

In other circumstances, directors are sometimes requested to enter into contractual commitments on a personal basis. For example if shares in the company are being sold on a takeover (particularly if the company is a comparatively small one) or where finance is being obtained for the company, the directors may be requested to give personal warranties as to the current financial position of the company. Directors need to consider very carefully before giving such warranties and also the limitations which should be imposed if they do decide to give such warranties. Where a director also has a substantial shareholding in the company, then he obviously has a personal interest which may justify him giving such warranties. However in the case of a non-executive director who has no shareholding in the company, his financial interest in giving such warranties is fairly limited.

CHAPTER 15

Directors and insolvency

15.1 Introduction

From the point of view of directors' responsibilities, undoubtedly one of the most difficult situations arises when the company is experiencing financial problems. Often it will be clear that it is simply a temporary down-turn in business or slowness in collecting debts or something of that nature and the directors will justifiably be confident that the situation will be remedied in the near future. However on occasions the position may appear more serious and the future may look less clear, and it is here that the directors must consider their responsibilities very carefully. If they do not, and the company later goes into liquidation, the directors could find themselves personally liable in respect of debts of the company, if they have not acted appropriately.

There are two statutory provisions which can impose personal liability on directors in such situations. The first is fraudulent trading, and the second is wrongful trading. The two provisions exist side by side, wrongful trading having been introduced in recent years because of the difficulty in proving fraudulent trading. Under wrongful trading, honesty on its own is not a defence to a director.

15.2 Fraudulent trading

Fraudulent trading arises if any business of a company is carried on with intent to defraud creditors of the company (or creditors of any other person) or for any fraudulent purpose. There are two possible consequences of fraudulent trading:

Criminal offence
(a) Any person (including a director) who is a party to fraudulent trading is guilty of a criminal offence and imprisonment can be imposed as a penalty.

Liability for debts
(b) Any person (including a director) who is party to fraudulent trading can also be required to contribute to the assets of the company such amount (without limit) as the court orders.

Fraudulent trading is a serious matter and to come within the provisions of fraudulent trading there has to be some element of actual dishonesty or real moral blame. Clearly if a company obtains goods on credit when it knows there is no prospect of paying the supplier, that would be fraudulent trading. One single transaction can constitute fraudulent trading.

It will normally be inferred that there was dishonesty if a company continues to carry on business and incurs debts at a time when, to the knowledge of the directors, there was no reasonable prospect of the company ever paying those debts. However, to be liable some active participation is necessary on a director's part – this is inferred from the requirement that liability only arises if the director is a "party to" the fraudulent trading.

In nearly all cases fraudulent trading would also constitute wrongful trading and therefore the steps and actions which a director should take are dealt with below in relation to wrongful trading.

15.3 Wrongful trading

Wrongful trading arises where:
(a) the company has gone into insolvent liquidation;
(b) at some time before the actual liquidation a director knew or ought to have concluded that there was no reasonable prospect that the company would avoid going into insolvent liquidation;
(c) from the time that the director should have concluded (or did conclude) there was no such prospect, the director failed to take every step with a view to minimising the potential loss to the company's creditors.

In essence therefore what is envisaged is this. As soon as a director concludes (or should have concluded) that there is no prospect of avoiding insolvent liquidation, the director must take every step to minimise the loss to creditors, and if he does not do so, then the statute provides that he can be ordered to contribute to the assets of the company such amount (without limit) as the court decides.

In deciding what facts and conclusions should have been known or reached by a director and the steps which he ought to take, the director is assumed to be a reasonably diligent person who has the general knowledge, skill and experience that may reasonably be expected of a person carrying out the same functions as are entrusted to that director in relation to the company and (if greater) the general knowledge, skill and experience which that particular director actually has. One has to consider therefore the role which is entrusted to the director within the company, the general knowledge, skill and experience which one would reasonably expect someone performing that role within that company to have and, if the person actually has greater knowledge and experience, then one takes that into account as well.

As will be seen from the above, the key factor is at what date a director concluded (or should have concluded) that there was no reasonable prospect of the company avoiding going into insolvent liquidation. It is from that date that the director's duty to take every step with a view to minimising the potential loss to the company's creditors arises. If he does not realise the inevitability of the insolvent liquidation when he should have realised and fails from then on to take every step to minimise the loss to creditors, then he can be made personally liable.

There have so far been few reported court decisions on wrongful trading, but some points which have arisen are these. It is no defence to a director to show that he acted honestly. The fact that a director was honest will not mean that only a very small contribution to the assets of the company will be required. All factors will be taken into account in determining the final amount of contribution, including, for example the conduct of the director and the effect on the position of creditors. The provision is intended to be compensatory. The fact that the company is in arrears with its accounts (resulting in the director not appreciating the financial problems) is no defence since it is the directors' duty to make sure proper accounts are available. Finally, the court cannot grant relief to a director from his liability (see 7.2 above).

15.4 General precautions to take in advance

What steps then should a prudent director take in advance to guard against personal liability for fraudulent or wrongful trading? Clearly, much must depend on the nature of the company and the circumstances generally, but the following suggestions are made.

At all times, the following steps would be sensible:

Appropriate qualifications/experience
(a) Because, under wrongful trading, a director is judged partly by the knowledge, skill and judgment reasonably expected of someone undertaking the director's functions, a director should think carefully before taking on a directorship, particularly specific executive responsibilities, if he thinks he may not have the appropriate qualifications or experience to undertake those functions properly.

Necessary attention
(b) The responsibility for wrongful or fraudulent trading will usually differentiate between the roles which directors have in a company, as between, for example, a non-executive non-professional director on the one hand and a full-time professionally qualified executive director on the other hand. However whatever the role the director has, he should make sure that he devotes the time and

attention to it which is reasonably to be expected and that he does consider carefully any accounts or other documents or information which he receives. Also, whatever his role, he should consider whether there is other information which he should be receiving and if so, request it. Also he should make every reasonable effort to attend board meetings.

Board meetings
(c) Particularly in the case of smaller companies, there is sometimes a tendency not to have board meetings of any regular nature. Consideration should therefore be given to having regular board meetings, the regularity depending on the size and nature of the business. This is the best way for directors to keep themselves informed of all aspects of the company's affairs rather than just those which exist in their day-to-day duties.

Accounting information
(d) The directors should ensure that they have proper accounting records and up to date accounting information – again the extent and timing of this must depend on the individual company, but directors will be expected to have available reasonably up to date accounting information when fulfilling their functions.

15.5 Steps to take when financial problems arise

If the company appears to be starting to experience financial difficulties, then obviously directors have to bear in mind their responsibilities referred to in 15.2 and 15.3 above, and they have to be considering whether there is any reasonable prospect of avoiding insolvent liquidation. They should:
(a) Consider taking professional advice.
(b) Bear in mind that directors of a public company have to call an extraordinary general meeting if the net assets fall below 50% of paid-up share capital – see 23.5 below.
(c) Consider what ways may be open to the company to improve its financial position, and the possibilities of injecting further capital (though obviously potential financiers would need to be fully informed of the company's financial position).
(d) Make sure that they have frequent board meetings to consider and review the financial position of the company. The minutes of those meetings should carefully note the considerations which the directors took into account, assuming they reach a decision to carry on business. If the directors have received professional advice that suggests they may have reached the stage where

insolvent liquidation is inevitable, then obviously they will need to be considering their position very carefully indeed before acting against such advice.
(e) As mentioned above, when insolvent liquidation is inevitable, directors have to take every step with a view to minimising loss to creditors. Again professional advice will be appropriate as to what steps should be taken.

If an individual director considers that the stage of inevitable insolvent liquidation has been reached, then obviously it is essential to raise this immediately with the other directors of the company. If however they do not share the same view, then the director will have to consider the following steps:
(a) Convening a meeting of the board of directors to consider the point specifically and, if necessary, insisting that his views are noted in the minutes of the meeting.
(b) As indicated, it is the duty of the director to take every step to minimise the loss to creditors. If he simply resigns as a director immediately, then he will probably not have taken every possible step. Before resigning therefore a director should seek professional advice on whether there is any further step he should take or can take.

15.6 Transactions once the company becomes "insolvent"

Obviously directors must not pay away monies or enter into transactions deliberately to defraud creditors and they would, apart from personal liability for the loss to the company, be potentially criminally liable if they did so. However when a company goes into liquidation, transactions entered into within a certain period prior to the liquidation can be reviewed and may be set aside. Also, directors who enter into such transactions may, particularly if one of their number benefited or if it is not possible to recover the monies from the third party, be personally liable to make good any loss to the company as a result of the transaction.

The transactions in question are those known as transactions at an undervalue, voidable preferences and voidable floating charges. All of these transactions potentially have the effect of putting a creditor in a better position than he would have been if all creditors had been treated equally.

Transaction at an undervalue
(a) A "transaction at an undervalue" is one where the company does not obtain adequate consideration for the transaction, though there is a defence if it is shown that the transaction was entered

into in good faith and that at the time there were reasonable grounds for believing the transaction would benefit the company. An example of a transaction at an undervalue would be a charge or security created in favour of an existing creditor for an existing debt.

Voidable preference
(b) A "voidable preference" arises where a creditor (or someone who has guaranteed the company's debts) is given some advantage over other creditors, but for the provision to apply the company must be influenced by a desire to give that creditor (or guarantor) preference over others. An example of a preference would be paying a creditor money which was due, when there were many other debts of the company outstanding, unless there was a clear advantage to the company in paying off that particular creditor. If that creditor was pursuing legal proceedings against the company it may be to the company's advantage to have those proceedings terminated but the fact of proceedings will not be conclusive to prove there was no intention to prefer. Another common example of a voidable preference is where directors have given personal guarantees to the company's bank and, immediately prior to liquidation, they ensure that payments are made to reduce the overdraft, so "preferring" both the bank and, ultimately, themselves (as guarantors) to the detriment of other creditors.

Voidable floating charge
(c) A "voidable floating charge" is, broadly speaking, where the company creates a floating charge in favour of a creditor as security for an existing debt. By giving security in this way the company is effectively preferring the creditor (compared with other creditors who are not given security). The floating charge is only voidable to the extent it secures existing debts and it can be effective in relation to any new monies which are lent by the creditor.

Effect of the transactions
In relation to all the above transactions, the starting point for deciding whether the transaction can be set aside is whether at the time the transaction is entered into or the payment made, the company was technically insolvent (or became so as a result). For this purpose the company is insolvent if any of the following apply:
 (a) if the company is unable to pay its debts as they fall due;
 (b) if the value of the company's assets is less than that of its liabilities (including contingent liabilities);

(c) if a formal written demand has been served on the company at its registered office requiring payment of a debt of more than £750 and the debt remains unpaid after 21 days;
(d) if a creditor has obtained court judgment and has attempted to enforce it by legal process against the company's assets without success.

As indicated, the important factor is whether the company is insolvent at the time. If so, the transaction can be set aside if liquidation (or an administration followed by a liquidation) follows within a certain period. The relevant period is generally two years for a transaction at an undervalue, six months for a voidable preference and 12 months for a voidable floating charge. However, where the creditor or person preferred is "connected" with the company (which includes directors, their relations or controlled companies) presumptions are made (unless the contrary is shown) that there was an intention to prefer or that the company was insolvent, and in such cases of voidable preference the period within which any such transaction can be set aside is extended from six months to two years prior to liquidation.

Directors must therefore be very careful of such transactions if the company is insolvent, and particularly so if the transaction in any way benefits them or persons connected with them.

15.7 Position once liquidation inevitable

Once liquidation seems inevitable, if they have not already done so, directors would be well advised to take appropriate advice. As indicated in **15.3** above, they have a duty to take *every step* to minimise loss to creditors. This is balanced by a corresponding duty to ensure that creditors are treated fairly. Directors must therefore ensure that all assets of the company are preserved and that no creditor is able to take any unfair advantage. Matters and steps which the directors will need to take and consider will depend on all the circumstances, but may include the following:
(a) Deciding on the method to put the company into liquidation. There is also the alternative of applying to the court for an administration order as opposed to liquidation, if for example it is thought that assets can be more beneficially realised in this way. Advice would obviously be necessary on this.
(b) Discussing with any secured creditor whether it is appropriate for the secured creditor to appoint a receiver.
(c) Suspending the company's trading activities.
(d) Considering the position of employees and the termination of their employment.

(e) Preserving the company's assets, which will include avoiding any creditor or third party taking these. For example, creditors may claim retention of title rights, but directors should not permit goods to be taken, without advice, pending liquidation. To do so could amount to a voidable preference if it turns out there was no valid retention of title.
(f) If the company is still receiving cash or cheques, the directors will need to consider operating a separate bank account, otherwise to pay the money into an overdrawn account may amount to a voidable preference (particularly if it is guaranteed by a director). If the money is for goods or services not yet supplied, this will need to be retained separately otherwise it could constitute wrongful trading.
(g) If there are any goods or services which are being supplied to the company and are essential, cash will have to be provided, otherwise this could amount to wrongful trading.
(h) Subject to advice, any further payments out of the company's bank account will have to be stopped.

15.8 Liquidation

There are two methods of putting a company into liquidation. The first is known as compulsory liquidation in which a petition is made to the court for a winding-up order. A creditor can petition, so also can the company and also the directors themselves provided they are unanimous.

The other method of putting a company into liquidation is voluntary liquidation. Where the company is solvent, the members can pass a resolution to wind up the company provided the directors have first made a written declaration that the company is able to pay its debts. If, however, the company is insolvent, the directors have to call a meeting of shareholders (who must pass an extraordinary resolution) and a meeting of creditors to put the company into liquidation and appoint a liquidator. Not less than seven days' notice must be given to creditors of a creditors' meeting and it must be advertised and state where information regarding the company's affairs can be obtained. At the creditors' meeting the directors must present a statement of affairs of the company in the required form, and if the directors fail to do so, then it is an offence.

Once the company is in liquidation, the directors' functions as directors cease but the directors must co-operate fully with the liquidator in all necessary respects.

15.9 Misfeasance

Reference is sometimes made to misfeasance proceedings. Where a company is in liquidation, the liquidator is able to make use of a speedier procedure against any director who has been guilty of misfeasance, "misfeasance" simply meaning any misapplication of money or property or any other breach of duty relating to the company.

15.10 Disqualification of directors

A director can be disqualified from acting as a director or taking part in the management of a company for a particular period if he has been guilty of any serious offence relating to the conduct of a company or if, for example, he has persistently been in default in relation to provisions of the companies legislation requiring returns, accounts or other documents to be filed at the Companies' Registry. In particular he will be conclusively regarded as having been persistently in default if he has been found guilty (whether or not on the same occasion) of three or more such defaults.

These provisions about disqualification apply at any time. However there are special provisions dealing with disqualification where a company has gone into insolvent liquidation. In such a case a director can be disqualified if his conduct as a director of that company is regarded as making him unfit to be concerned in the management of any company. Matters that are taken into account in deciding this are the extent of the director's responsibility for the causes of the company becoming insolvent or his responsibility for entering into transactions at an undervalue or voidable preferences. Only the Secretary of State can apply for such an order, and only if he considers it "expedient in the public interest", but in every liquidation the liquidator must make a report to the Secretary of State if he thinks such a course is appropriate. The concept of "unfitness" is potentially very wide-ranging.

It should be noted that if a person acts in the management of a company while disqualified he can be personally liable for the debts of the company incurred during such period. In the same way a person who acts in the management of a company on the instructions of a disqualified person can himself be personally liable. It needs to be appreciated that a disqualification order does not simply prevent one being a director of another company – it also prevents one taking any part in the "management" of another company.

15.11 Restrictions on re-use of company name

Because of the practice of unscrupulous businessmen allowing a company to run up debts and go into liquidation, and then starting to carry on the same business through a new company under the same or a similar name, restrictions were introduced to prevent this. If a company goes into insolvent liquidation, any person who was a director within the preceding 12 months, may not within five years afterwards be a director or otherwise concerned in any company or business which is known by the same or a similar name to the company in liquidation. Not only is it a criminal offence to do so, but the director is personally liable for the debts of the new company during the relevant period.

CHAPTER 16

Accounts, finance and taxation

16.1 Accounting records

The directors have a duty to ensure that the company keeps proper accounting records. The accounting records must be sufficient to show and explain the company's transactions. They must disclose the company's financial position with reasonable accuracy at any time, and must enable the directors to ensure that any balance sheet and profit and loss account prepared in respect of the company comply with the requirements of the Companies Acts.

In particular the accounting records must contain entries from day to day of details of all sums received and paid by the company and a record of the company's assets and liabilities.

If the company's business includes dealing in goods, the accounting records must contain statements of stock held at the end of the financial year, stocktaking records, and, except in relation to retail sales, statements of all goods sold and purchased, showing the goods, the buyer and the seller in sufficient detail to enable them to be identified.

The accounting records have to be kept at the registered office or at such other place as the directors decide, and are open to inspection at all times by the company's directors.

In the case of a private company, these accounting records must be kept and retained for at least three years after they have been made and in the case of a public company, for at least six years. (However in practice it will be desirable to keep these records for longer – for tax purposes the Revenue generally have six years in which to make assessments (longer in some cases) and records for VAT purposes must be kept for at least six years).

In default of compliance by a company with the statutory requirements, the directors themselves may find they are liable to imprisonment in the worse case, or to a fine, or both.

Also, it is a serious criminal offence for any person dishonestly to destroy, conceal or falsify accounts or records or to use any such accounts or records knowing them to be false or misleading.

16.2 Management accounts

As is mentioned below, the directors have a duty to prepare annual audited accounts. Although the preparation of internal management accounts is not a requirement of the Companies Acts as such, it would be difficult for directors to be able to perform their legal duties as a director without these. Furthermore, from a purely practical point of view directors would be operating at a very considerable disadvantage if they did not have up to date financial information regarding the company when making their decisions, particularly if there is danger of insolvency.

It is advisable therefore for directors to ensure that internal management accounts are prepared at regular intevals, eg monthly or perhaps quarterly, depending on the nature of the company and its size. The directors should discuss this aspect with their auditors.

16.3 Requirement for audited accounts

Every company has to notify the Registrar of Companies of its accounting reference date. This must be notified within six months of the date of the company's incorporation, otherwise the accounting reference date will automatically be the 31st March (in the case of a company incorporated after the coming into force of the Companies Act 1989, it will be the anniversary of incorporation). The first accounting reference period of the company must be not less than six months nor longer than 18 months ending on its accounting reference date. Each successive accounting reference period runs from the end of one accounting reference period to the next accounting reference date.

A company can subsequently alter its accounting reference date, but generally any such alteration has to be made before the expiry of the accounting reference period which is then current; however any such change must not extend the current accounting reference period to more than 18 months.

The Companies Acts require directors to prepare a profit and loss account for each accounting reference period and a balance sheet as at the end of the financial year. The Acts lay down very detailed requirements as to the form and content of such accounts. Overall, the balance sheet is to provide a true and fair view of the state of affairs of the company at the end of the year and the profit and loss account must give a true and fair view of the profit or loss of the company for that year. It is not possible to set out in detail here the requirements of the Acts regarding the form and contents of accounts, and directors will need to discuss these with their auditors. There are modified requirements for small and medium sized companies which meet certain criteria as regards turnover, balance sheet total and numbers of employees.

The accounts must have attached to them a directors' report which must contain a fair view of the development of the business of the company for the year and the amount (if any) which the directors propose to recommend as a dividend as well as other detailed requirements.

For listed companies, still more detailed requirements are laid down by the Stock Exchange.

The company's annual accounts must be audited by independent professional auditors, and the auditors have to prepare a report on the accounts as to whether they have been properly prepared in accordance with the Companies Acts and whether they show a true and fair view of the company's affairs and its profit or loss for the year.

The company's auditors have a right of access at all times to the company's books, accounts and vouchers and are entitled to require from the company's officers such information and explanations as they think necessary. The auditors have to state in their report if they consider proper accounting records have not been kept by the company.

It is an offence for a director or officer of the company knowingly or recklessly to give information to the auditors which is false, misleading or deceptive in any material respect.

16.4 Time limit for laying and filing accounts

The directors are under a duty to "lay before the company in general meeting" accounts for each financial year. The auditor's report is to be read out before the company in general meeting and a copy of the accounts must be delivered to the Registrar of Companies. (However see 24.5 below as regards the power for private companies to dispense with this).

In the case of a private company, the period for laying and delivering accounts is within 10 months after the end of the relevant accounting reference period, and in the case of a public company, within seven months after the end of the relevant accounting reference period.

It should be noted however that when a company's first accounting reference period begins on the date of its incorporation and is a period of more than 12 months, the period otherwise allowed is reduced by the number of days by which the relevant accounting reference period is longer than 12 months, but this does not require the accounts to be delivered earlier than three months after the end of the accounting reference period.

If the company fails to lay and deliver the accounts as above, then any person who was a director of the company immediately before the end of the relevant period is guilty of an offence and liable to a fine (which may mount daily while the default persists); however, it is a defence for a director to prove that he took all reasonable steps for ensuring compliance. A similar provision applies if the accounts which are laid and delivered do not comply with the requirements of the Companies Acts.

If the company fails to lay and deliver its accounts as above, and the directors fail to make good the default within 14 days of notice served on them, the court, on the application of any member or creditor or the Registrar of Companies, may make an order directing the directors to make good the default within such time as may be specified, and the court may order the directors to pay the costs of the application.

16.5 Auditors

Every company must appoint auditors (unless it is "dormant" during the whole financial year in question – ie it has no significant accounting transactions and it passes an appropriate shareholders' resolution). The directors can appoint the first auditors or fill a casual vacancy, but basically the company appoints (or re-appoints) the auditors each year at the annual general meeting. (However see **24.5** below as regards the power for private companies to dispense with this requirement.)

Auditors must be professionally qualified accountants and a director or employee of the company cannot also act as auditor nor can a partner of a director or employee.

Auditors can be removed by an ordinary resolution of the company but 28 days' notice must be given to the company of an intention to propose such a resolution. An auditor who is proposed to be removed then has similar rights to a director proposed to be removed to request representations to be circulated to shareholders, etc (see **26.4** below).

An auditor may resign at any time, but his resignation is not effective unless it contains a statement that there are no circumstances connected with his resignation which he considers should be brought to the notice of members or creditors (or, a statement of such circumstances). A copy of the resignation has to be filed at the Companies Registry, and if there is a statement of circumstances, a copy has to be sent to all members.

16.6 Error in audited accounts

Very occasionally, an error or problem may come to light in respect of audited accounts after the time they have been sent to shareholders and before the annual general meeting. It is essential that directors take immediate advice if this does arise, since it is an offence to lay defective accounts before members, and there could be worse repercussions if the error led to dividends being paid out of capital or the like.

The Companies Act 1989 is introducing new provisions providing for directors to prepare revised accounts where the original accounts did not comply with the statutory requirements. The Secretary of State is also given power to question whether a company's accounts comply with the statutes.

16.7 Corporation tax

Companies pay corporation tax on their profits and capital gains. In calculating what are the taxable profits of a company more or less the same provisions apply as apply in the case of individual traders, but in the case of companies they are taxed in respect of any given financial year by reference to their profits for that same financial year (not on the profits of the preceding year).

The financial year for corporation tax purposes is the year from 1st April to 31st March (unlike the income tax year which runs from 6th April to 5th April), and the rate of corporation tax is set for each financial year.

Corporation tax for any financial year is charged on the profits of the company arising in that financial year. However assessments to corporation tax are made on a company by reference to its accounting period (ie the period of its audited accounts), and the chargeable amount of the profits is, where necessary, apportioned between the financial years in which the accounting period falls. This would be necessary where the rates of corporation tax differ in the relevant financial years.

Corporation tax is generally payable within nine months of the end of the accounting period or, if later, within 30 days of the notice of assessment.

The rate of corporation tax currently is 35 per cent, but in the case of "small" companies the rate is 25 per cent. "Small" companies means companies with profits for the year of up to £100,000. Where a company's profits fall between £100,000 and £500,000 there are transitional provisions. The "small" companies tax rate does not apply to close investment-holding companies – these are basically defined as companies which are not part of a trading group nor property investment companies which let properties to third parties.

Companies which are resident in the United Kingdom are liable to corporation tax on all their profits (including overseas profits, but subject to certain relief in respect of overseas taxes paid), whereas companies which are not resident in the United Kingdom are only taxable in the United Kingdom on profits derived from a branch or agency in the United Kingdom. Residence for corporation tax purposes used to be decided by where control of the company was exercised (often in practice meaning where meetings of the board of directors were held). This still applies in the case of companies incorporated outside the United Kingdom, but since 1988 all companies incorporated in the United Kingdom are treated as resident here for corporation tax purposes. Transitional provisions apply where a UK incorporated company had been non-resident prior to 1988.

If a company has received a dividend from another UK resident company then the dividend is regarded as "franked investment income" and is not further liable to corporation tax in the hands of the receiving company.

Close companies

There are special provisions which apply to certain companies (known as "close companies") which are designed to prevent tax avoidance. The definition of close companies is complex, but generally can be said to apply where a company is under the control of five or fewer shareholders (or "participators"). Up until 1989 it was possible for the Revenue to apportion certain of the income of a close company among its shareholders and to tax them at higher rate tax on the amount apportioned. However these apportionment provisions have now been abolished so that the special provisions now applying to close companies are of limited application, basically as follows:
   (a) if a close company provides benefits or facilities to any shareholder or participator (except an employee or director whose benefits would be taxable anyway), then it is treated as a distribution (dividend);
   (b) if a close company makes a loan to a shareholder/participator (or his associate) then the company is treated as making a distribution.

16.8 Advance corporation tax

When a company pays a dividend, it has to pay advance corporation tax. The rate of advance corporation tax is generally linked with the basic rate of income tax of individuals, as explained below. The rate is currently 25/75ths based on the current standard rate of individual income tax of 25 per cent.

Advance corporation tax works in this way. If a company pays a dividend of £750, it has to pay advance corporation tax of 25/75ths of the amount, ie £250. This advance corporation tax is payable to the Revenue but can be set against the company's liability to corporation tax on its profits. So far as the shareholder is concerned in the above example, he will have received a payment by way of dividend of £750. This is treated as if it was a payment net of basic rate income tax, ie he is treated as if he had received a gross dividend of £1,000 less basic rate income tax of 25 per cent, producing a net dividend of £750. If the shareholder is, by virtue of his other income, liable to higher rate tax then he will have to pay that higher rate tax based on the gross dividend of £1,000.

CHAPTER 17

Administration

17.1 Documents and records to be available for inspection

Companies are required to maintain certain documents and records and to make these available for inspection by various interested parties. The extent to which these are to be available for inspection varies according to the standing of the party in question, and for this purpose four separate categories can conveniently be recognised:

Directors
(a) The directors themselves have a general right of access to all the company's books of account at any time and without any need to give notice.

Shareholders
(b) The company's shareholders have only limited rights of access to the company's records. In the case of a private company, where the rights of the shareholders are regulated by a shareholders' or joint venture agreement, there is often provision for the shareholders themselves to have a general right of access to the company's books and records, to which the company (if it is a party to the agreement) will be bound, but in the absence of an express contractual provision of this kind shareholders' rights are very limited. They have a general right of inspection of the statutory books and minutes of shareholders' meetings (but not directors' meetings); the annual audited accounts must be sent to each shareholder and, in addition, laid before the shareholders at the annual general meeting; and there is a right to inspect directors' service contracts with the company or its subsidiaries (or, where there is no written contract, a written memorandum of its terms) but this only applies to service contracts with an unexpired term of more than 12 months or which cannot be terminated by the company without compensation during the next following 12 months.

The standard articles state that no member shall have any right of inspecting the accounting records or other books or documents of the company except as conferred by statute or authorised by the directors or by ordinary resolution of the company.

Public bodies
(c) Certain public bodies and officials such as, in particular, the Inland Revenue and Customs and Excise or inspectors appointed by the Department of Trade to investigate a company's affairs, have specific powers allowing them to inspect relevant documents and records.

General public
(d) The general public have a right under the Companies Acts to inspect the various statutory registers maintained by the company, in addition to their right to inspect the documents on public record at the Companies Registry in respect of the company.

17.2 Statutory books

A company is required by the Companies Acts to keep various statutory registers, namely:

A register of its members
(a) This must contain the names and addresses of the shareholders, with details of the shares or stock held and the amount of capital paid (or agreed to be considered as paid) on those shares, details of different classes of shares held (where relevant), and the dates on which shareholders are first registered as such and cease to be shareholders. If the company has more than 50 members, the names of the members should be indexed.

A register of directors and secretaries
(b) This should include all names (including former names) and home addresses; and, in the case of directors, their nationality, business occupation and other directorships currently held or held at any time during the previous five years (other than wholly-owned subsidiaries and group companies and dormant companies). Where a company is subject to a statutory age limit for directors (broadly, public companies and their subsidiaries), the date of birth of the directors should also be recorded

A register of directors' interests in shares and debentures of the company and of other group companies
(c) The company must keep up-to-date a register of all such interests which directors are required to notify in writing (see **12.1** above) and are notified, although it should be noted that the obligation

to register certain events arises regardless of whether the individual director concerned has complied with his obligation to notify the company of that event or not.

A register of charges
(d) A company is required to keep a register of all charges over the company's property (including any floating charges over the company's undertaking or any of its property), giving a short description of the property charged, the amount of the charge and (except in the case of bearer securities) the names of those entitled to the benefit of it.

Normally, it will be the job of the secretary to ensure that the registers are kept up-to-date and in accordance with the Act, but any director may, along with the company itself, be liable for a fine if the director is himself "in default". There is provision in most cases for the amount of the fine to increase daily while the default persists, so that it could, prove to be substantial. The necessary registers are conveniently available from most law stationers, either in bound or loose-leaf form and also incorporating certain other registers which companies customarily keep for ease of reference but which are not required to be kept by law – namely, a register of share allotments, a register of transfers of shares, a register to record use of the company seal and a register of debentures. Note that, although a register of debentures is not required to be kept, if the company does issue debentures and accordingly keeps a register, that register is itself subject to regulation under the Act.

The register of directors and secretaries and the register of charges are to be kept at the registered office, but the register of members may be kept elsewhere if the work of maintaining it is done elsewhere and notice is given to Companies House. The register of directors' share interests should be kept in the same place as the register of members.

17.3 Filing documents at Companies House

There are a very large range of matters which are required to be notified to Companies House, though many of them in practice arise only rarely and will not affect the average company. Details are required to be completed on the "prescribed forms", which are available either from law stationers for a small charge, or free, on written request only, from the Stationery Section at Companies House. The forms will need to be signed by (in most cases) either the secretary or one director, and sent to the Registrar of Companies at Companies House, where they will be transferred to microfiche and placed on the public register. There are time limits for filing the forms, which vary according to the matter to be notified. It is helpful to note that the number of the form corresponds with the equivalent section of the Companies Act 1985 requiring the details in question to be notified. Details of some of the more common forms are shown in Appendix B.

In addition to the details required to be given on the prescribed forms, the passing of certain shareholders' resolutions must also be notified to Companies House. This applies to all special resolutions, extraordinary resolutions and elective resolutions, and to a limited number of ordinary resolutions – in particular, an ordinary resolution increasing the authorised share capital, or authorising the directors to allot shares. The time limit is 15 days.

As with the keeping of the statutory registers, normally the secretary will undertake responsibility for filing the necessary forms and papers, but again, a director – if he is "in default" – can be liable along with the company and can be subject to a fine (in most cases with the possibility of a default fine increasing daily).

In practice there is a time delay between the time that documents are lodged at the Registry and the time at which they become available for inspection since the documents first have to be microfilmed. In the case of certain time-critical documents, such as mortgages or insolvency documents, a note is made on the microfiche to show that there are documents which have been lodged.

If a company does not give notice of certain changes or events then its position may be prejudiced as against third parties (who as a result may not know of the event in question). The events concerned are the making of a winding-up order or the appointment of a liquidator, any alteration of the company's memorandum or articles of association, any change in the company's directors, or any change in the situation of the company's registered office. The company cannot rely on any such change or event to avoid a liability to a third party unless *either* the company can show that the person was actually aware of them *or* the Registrar of Companies, having been duly notified of the events, has published formal notice in the London Gazette or Edinburgh Gazette. The company may also not be able to rely on them within 15 days after they have been officially notified if the third party concerned was unavoidably prevented from knowing of the event at that time.

Under the Companies Act 1989 (when it is in force) a change of the company's registered office takes effect upon registration by the Registrar but documents can still be served on the company at its previous registered office for 14 days thereafter.

17.4 Company stationery and documents

By statute there are strict rules designed to ensure that people dealing with the company are aware of the fact that it is a limited liability company which they are dealing with, and to ensure that they can readily identify the company in question.

The directors must ensure that all letters and order forms of the company have the following details on them:

(a) The name of the company, including the word Limited (or Ltd) or the words Public Limited Company (or plc). A company with its registered office in Wales may use the Welsh equivalent. Certain non-profit making companies can obtain exemption from the requirement to use the word "limited" as part of their name, but they must nonetheless state on letters and order forms that they are a limited company.

(b) Place of registered office (eg England and Wales or Scotland) and its registered number.

(c) The address of its registered office.

(d) It is not necessary to state the share capital of the company, but if this is stated, then it must refer to the actual paid up share capital.

(e) It is not necessary to state the names of the directors, but if they are stated then the christian name (or initials) and surname of every director of the company (or the name of any corporate director) must be stated (though this does not apply if the name of a director is merely stated in the text of a letter or as a signatory to a letter).

(f) In the case of certain investment companies, the fact that it is such an investment company.

In addition to the requirements in respect of letters and order forms, the full name of the company must be shown in all notices and official publications, in all bills of exchange, promissory notes, endorsements, cheques and orders for money or goods and in all its invoices, receipts and letters of credit. A director can be personally liable if he signs a bill of exchange, promissory note, cheque or order for money or goods without stating the full name of the company.

17.5 Places of business

Every company is obliged to have its name on the outside of every office or place in which its business is carried on. The name must appear in a conspicuous position and in letters which are easily legible. It is an offence not to display the company's name in this manner and both the company and a director who is in default are liable to a fine.

17.6 Company secretary

Every company must have a company secretary and the same person cannot be both company secretary and a *sole* director of the company, but there is no objection to a person being one of two or more directors and also company secretary. In the case of a public limited company (but not a private company) it is the duty of the directors to ensure that the person appointed secretary is a person who appears to them to have the requisite knowledge and experience to act as secretary and who is either suitably professionally qualified (ie a barrister, advocate, solicitor, accountant or chartered secretary) or a person who has held the office of secretary previously for a certain time or who appears to the directors to have the necessary knowledge to hold such a position.

When an act is required to be done both by a director and the secretary, a person who is both director and secretary cannot do it on his own.

Although accepted as a general administrative function, the scope of the job of secretary depends on the particular company. In most companies, the secretary assumes the primary responsibility for ensuring compliance with Companies Registry filing and ensuring that the statutory registers are kept up-to-date. He would also deal with matters such as preparing minutes of directors' and shareholders' meetings, sending notices and other documents to shareholders and similar administrative matters. A secretary is normally also one of the persons empowered by the articles to witness the use of the company seal, depending on what the articles say. What other functions the secretary also performs depends on the particular company. In some companies the role may be fairly limited (dealing with the purely formal statutory requirements) whereas in other companies the secretary may be given much wider executive functions, including responsibility for personnel, accounting systems and general administration.

Normally under the articles, the secretary is appointed and removed and the terms of his appointment are determined by the board of directors.

The company secretary is an officer of the company and is responsible with the directors for ensuring that the requirements of the Companies Acts are complied with.

17.7 Company seal

Up until now every company has been required to have a company seal, or "common seal", on which should be engraved its name in legible characters, and a company may also, for convenience, have a separate seal for use for sealing securities issued by the company, being a copy of the company's common seal with the addition of the word "securities". In practice, almost all companies will have a seal, but the Companies Act 1989 will remove this requirement. Companies will be able to execute deeds by the signature of a director and the secretary, if it is expressed to be executed by the company and it is clear on the face of it that it is intended to take effect as a deed.

The articles will normally provide that the seal may be used only with the authority of the directors, or a committee of directors which is itself so authorised. Usually the articles provide that the use of the seal is to be witnessed by the signatures of two directors, or by the secretary and another director, but large companies which frequently need to seal documents in the course of their business, or which have a large number of shareholders and accordingly are frequently issuing share certificates, may provide for other named officers to witness the use of the seal alone or jointly.

The kinds of document which are normally required to be executed as deeds under the company's seal are: transfers of freehold property, leases, share transfers by the company, mortgages, debentures, trust deeds (eg in respect of pension schemes or profit sharing schemes), share certificates and powers of attorney. Also, in the case of certain major contracts (eg building contracts) it is sometimes preferred that it should be executed under seal as a deed since this means that the limitation period (within which proceedings must be brought) is 12 years rather than the usual six years.

CHAPTER 18

Issue of shares

18.1 General

Until a few years ago there was no statutory control on the issue of share capital and in many cases directors were given complete authority by the articles to issue shares as they saw fit. However, regardless of what a company's articles may say, certain statutory requirements and controls have now been imposed in respect of the issue of share capital so as to give greater protection to existing shareholders. These statutory requirements are quite detailed, and before dealing with them, it may be helpful to summarise them very briefly:

Authority to issue shares
   (a) The actual issuing of shares is still carried out by the directors, but before directors can issue shares, statute now requires that the shareholders must first give authority to the directors to do so. This is dealt with in **18.4** below.

Pre-emption rights
   (b) A second statutory requirement is that when shares are to be issued for cash, the directors must offer the shares proportionately to existing shareholders unless these statutory requirements have been disapplied by the company in the manner mentioned in **18.5** below.

Non-cash consideration (public companies)
   (c) Thirdly, in the case of public companies, where shares are to be issued for a non-cash consideration, that non-cash consideration must be properly valued (subject to certain exceptions) as mentioned in **18.7** below.

18.2 Authorised share capital

A company can only issue shares if it has available sufficent authorised but unissued share capital. The initial amount of share capital which a company is authorised to issue is set out in the memorandum of association, but the company can at any time by ordinary resolution increase its authorised share capital. Accordingly once a company has issued all its initial share capital (for example the initial share capital may be expressed as "£100 divided into 100 ordinary shares of £1 each") then it must pass an ordinary resolution to increase the authorised share capital and create further shares which can be issued. A company can have as high or low an authorised share capital as it wishes (but public companies must have a minimum authorised and issued share capital of £50,000 – see 2.5 above), and can divide its shares into such nominal amounts as it thinks appropriate (eg 5p shares or £1 shares etc).

When a company increases its authorised share capital, it must file a copy of the resolution at the Companies Registry and file a form known as Notice of Increase of Capital.

18.3 Types of shares

A company can, if it wishes, create shares of different types and with differing share rights. The most usual type of share is the ordinary share, but a company can issue preference shares or deferred shares, or shares carrying such special dividend, voting or other rights as it thinks appropriate. Also, as mentioned in 20.2 below, it is now possible for a company to issue redeemable shares.

Apart from ordinary shares, preference shares are probably the most common type of share. They usually have a right to payment of a fixed dividend in priority to other shares, and in a winding-up they usually also have priority as regards repayment of share capital. Sometimes preference shares are only given restricted voting rights. However the precise rights given to any particular preference shares depend upon the articles of association or the terms on which the preference shares are issued.

18.4 Authority to issue shares

By statute directors are not allowed to issue any shares (other than shares subscribed for by the original subscribers to the memorandum of association or shares which are being allotted under an employees' share scheme) unless the directors have been authorised to issue the shares either (i) by an ordinary resolution of the shareholders, or (ii) by the company's articles of association. Such authority can either be a general authority to issue shares or an authority to issue shares on a particular occasion, but in either case the authority must state a maximum number of shares to which it applies, and must expire not later than five years after it is given (although for private companies the five year rule no longer applies if the shareholders pass an "elective resolution" – see 24.5 below). The company can renew the authority from time to time in the same way.

It must be emphasised that the authority must comply with these statutory requirements – a general power to directors to issue shares (without number or time limits, as used to appear in articles of association before the statutory provisions were introduced) is not sufficient.

18.5 Pre-emption rights on share issues

"Pre-emption rights" is the term given to the shareholders' right of first refusal to acquire other shares in that company, either when new shares are being issued or when one shareholder is selling out.

The statutory pre-emption rights
(a) In the case of an issue of new shares, even where the directors have authority to issue shares (**18.4** above), their right to do so is subject to pre-emption rights granted to shareholders by statute. Where a company is going to issue relevant equity shares (essentially this means shares other than fixed interest shares or shares under an employees' share scheme) *for cash* it must first offer the new shares proportionately to its existing ordinary shareholders and allow the time for such offer to expire before issuing the shares to anyone else. This provision does not apply where shares are to be issued wholly or partly for a consideration other than cash, eg in exchange for shares in another company on a take-over.

The statutory pre-emption provisions contain detailed rules as to the time the offer must be open for acceptance (not less than 21 days) and as to notices to be given to shareholders and other matters. If a company contravenes these provisions then the company and every officer who knowingly authorised or permitted the contravention are jointly liable to compensate any person to whom such an offer should have been made, for any loss or expense that person suffered.

Disapplying the statutory pre-emption rights
(b) Companies can, however, opt out of these statutory pre-emption provisions.
    (i) *Private companies*
        In the case of a private company, the statutory pre-emption provisions can be (and often are) entirely excluded by a suitable provision in the articles of association.
    (ii) *Public companies*
        In the case of a public company (or a private company which has not totally excluded the statutory pre-emption provisions) the statutory pre-emption provisions can be disapplied in the following manner:

(1) Where directors are *generally* authorised to issue shares (as per **18.4** above) then the company may by its articles or by special resolution give the directors power to allot shares as if the statutory pre-emption provisions did not apply (or can modify the statutory provisions).

(2) Alternatively, in *any* case where the directors are authorised to issue shares – either generally or for a particular occasion – the directors can be authorised by special resolution of the shareholders to issue shares for a *particular allotment* as if the statutory provisions did not apply to that allotment. However, where power is being obtained in relation to a particular allotment, it must be recommended by the directors and there must be circulated to the shareholders a written statement from the directors giving the reasons for their recommendation, the amount to be paid to the company in respect of the new shares, and the directors' justification of this amount. In making such a recommendation, directors have to bear in mind that if they knowingly (or recklessly) include any misleading, false or deceptive remark in their recommendation then they can be liable to serious penalties.

Even where a company is content to follow the basic pre-emption requirements, it is often convenient to obtain shareholder approval to disapply or modify these requirements, because the statutory requirements are not in all circumstances particularly convenient. For example, if a company has overseas shareholders with no UK address, notice has to be given in the Gazette to such shareholders under the statutory requirements.

In the case of companies whose shares are listed on the Stock Exchange, they have to comply with the additional requirements of the Stock Exchange in respect of pre-emption provisions.

18.6 Issues of shares for cash

It will be seen from this that before directors can issue shares for cash:
(a) they must first have authority as described in **18.4** above; and
(b) secondly, if they are not going to issue shares in accordance with the statutory pre-emption provisions, they must also have been exempted from these requirements as described in **18.5** above.

As regards the price at which shares should be issued for cash, by statute they cannot be issued at a price less than the nominal value of the shares. Also a public company cannot issue shares unless at least a quarter of the nominal value, and the whole of any premium, is paid up.

If shares are issued at a premium over their nominal value, then the amount of that premium has to be transferred to a share premium account and treated as capital.

A question that arises is whether directors have a duty to issue shares only at the full market value (including premium). Clearly, as in all other cases of directors exercising their powers, the directors must act in the best interests of the company as a whole, and it would potentially be a breach of their duty if they were to issue shares to themselves or their associates (or others) at what was manifestly less than the full market value of the shares. When offering shares proportionately to existing shareholders, directors will be wanting to set a reasonably attractive price to try and ensure that as many shareholders as possible take up the offer, and provided the price is not obviously unreasonable it is unlikely that any shareholder should have grounds for complaint if he has the opportunity to take up his proportion of shares at such a price. Where, however, directors are permitted to issue shares to outsiders, then it is part of their duty to try and obtain a suitable price for the shares. Directors should consider taking advice from the auditors as to the proper price, and if there is any doubt about the position, then it may be worth considering whether they should seek specific approval from the shareholders to the particular issue of shares on the terms proposed.

18.7 Issue of shares for non-cash consideration

Shares may also be issued for a consideration other than cash (or only partly for cash). As has been mentioned, where the consideration is not wholly cash, the statutory pre-emption provisions (**18.5** above) do not apply, and the directors can issue shares to anyone provided they are authorised in accordance with **18.4** above.

Private company
(a) In the case of a private company, there are no particular restrictions on the method of valuing the non-cash consideration nor the type of consideration – the directors must simply act *bona fide* and the consideration must not be clearly inadequate. Certainly, however, the directors must ensure that the shares are not effectively being issued at a discount (ie at a "price" less than their nominal value).

Public company
(b) In the case of a public company, there are various provisions and restrictions which apply when shares are issued for a non-cash consideration. In particular:
    (i) A public company cannot accept as consideration for shares an undertaking by any person to perform work or services for the company.
    (ii) A public company cannot accept as consideration for shares any undertaking which may be performed more than five years later.
    (iii) Subscribers' shares must be issued for cash, and there are certain restrictions on the number of shares which can be issued for non-cash consideration to a person who was a subscriber.
    (iv) A public company must not issue shares for a non-cash consideration unless an appropriately qualified independent valuer has valued the consideration within six months previously. However this does not apply to bonus issues or to takeovers on a share for share basis nor to arrangements whereby the assets and liabilities of a company are taken over by another in exchange for the issue of shares to the other company's shareholders – in such cases no valuation is required. There are detailed provisions regarding the valuation, and it is an offence for a director or anyone else to give materially false, misleading or deceptive information to such a valuer.

18.8 Directors' duties in respect of share issues

As in the case of the exercise of any power granted to the directors, they must exercise it in the best interests of the company, and not for any collateral purpose (eg simply to thwart a takeover) – **6.2-6.3** above.

18.9 Formalities in respect of share issues

Where shares are issued the following documents must be filed at the Companies Registry:
(a) a return of allotments stating the persons and number of shares which have been allotted and other details;
(b) if the consideration is a non-cash consideration a copy of the contract (or particulars of it) under which the shares are agreed to be allotted, together with a copy of the valuer's report, if applicable;

(c) if the company has increased its authorised share capital in order to create the necessary shares to issue, then it has to file a copy of the resolution and a Notice of Increase of Capital.

There is no longer any capital duty payable on the issue of shares.

18.10 Share certificates

By statute companies must issue share certificates within two months after the date on which the shares are issued.

CHAPTER 19

Financial assistance for acquisition of company's own shares

19.1 General prohibition

The basic rule is that where someone is proposing to acquire shares in a company (whether on first issue or purchase of the shares), it is illegal for the company itself to provide direct or indirect financial assistance to that person to enable him to do so (whether before or after he has acquired the shares). Financial assistance includes making gifts or loans, giving guarantees or providing security or the like. A typical example of providing financial assistance would be if a person purchases shares in a company with money borrowed from his bank, and the company in turn grants a mortgage over its assets as security for the purchaser's loan. The object of prohibiting such transactions generally is that they potentially reduce the company's assets (and hence creditor protection).

There are however certain exceptions to the general rule and these are described below.

19.2 General exceptions applying to all companies

Companies are permitted to give financial assistance for the acquisition of their own shares in certain limited circumstances. The principal exceptions are as follows:

(a) A lawful dividend (eg on a takeover the purchaser could subsequently take a lawfully permissible dividend and recoup some of the cost).

(b) A bonus issue (effectively a bonus issue is "paid for" out of the company's reserves or profits).

(c) Reductions of capital or a redemption or purchase of the company's shares under the statutory provisions (see chapter 20).

(d) A normal loan by a company where lending is part of its ordinary business.

(e) Providing financial assistance in connection with a *bona fide* employee share scheme.

(f) Making loans to *bona fide* employees (but not directors) to enable them to acquire shares in the company.

However in the case of a public company, items (d), (e) and (f) above are only permissible if any resulting reduction in net assets is covered by its distributable profits.

19.3 Additional exceptions applying to private companies

The main exception to the restriction on providing financial assistance relates to private companies since they are now permitted to provide financial assistance subject to the following conditions:
 (a) The net assets of the company must not be reduced by the financial assistance or, to the extent that they are reduced, the financial assistance must be provided out of distributable profits.
 (b) The arrangement must be approved by a special resolution of the company.
 (c) The directors must make a statutory declaration to the effect that the company will be solvent immediately following the giving of the financial assistance and will be able to pay its debts as they fall due over the next 12 months. The directors' declaration must have annexed to it an auditors' report that the auditors are not aware of anything to indicate that the opinion expressed by the directors is unreasonable. Dissenting shareholders holding 10% of any class of the company's share capital can apply to the court within 28 days of the special resolution to seek to cancel the resolution.

Also, once the procedures have been complied with, there are strict time limits within which the transaction must be carried out.

19.4 Directors' liability

If the company contravenes the restrictions on providing financial assistance for the acquisition of its shares then the company is guilty of an offence and likewise every director who is in default is guilty of an offence. Also, every director who was a party to any breach of the provisions would be in breach of his duties not to misapply the company's funds and could therefore be liable to the company for any loss suffered as a result of the transaction.

Also, in the case of the director's declaration referred to in **19.3** (c) above, a director is guilty of an offence if he makes such a declaration without reasonable grounds.

CHAPTER 20

Purchase by a company of its own shares: redeemable shares

20.1 Purchase by a company of its own shares

Until a few years ago it was not possible for a company to purchase its own shares. However it is now possible for a company to do so provided it is so authorised by its articles (the standard articles contain such a power).

Except in the case of private companies (see **20.3** below), the purchase monies must be provided out of the distributable profits of the company or out of the proceeds of a fresh issue of shares made for the purposes of the purchase. Also, shares can only be purchased if they are fully paid shares.

Different considerations apply depending upon whether the shares are to be purchased on a recognised Stock Exchange ("a market purchase") or not on a recognised Stock Exchange ("an off-market purchase"). Obviously a "market purchase" only applies to shares which are listed or dealt in on a recognised Stock Exchange (which includes shares traded on the Unlisted Securities Market).

Market purchase
 (a) A company can only make a market purchase of its own shares if it has been authorised to do so by an ordinary resolution of the shareholders. The ordinary resolution may be general or limited to the purchase of shares of a particular class or description, and it may be subject to conditions. However the authority *must* specify the maximum number of shares which may be acquired and determine both the maximum and minimum prices which may be paid for the shares and specify a date, not later than 18 months, on which the authority is to expire.

Off-market purchase
 (b) In the case of an off-market purchase the terms of the proposed contract must be approved in advance by special resolution of the shareholders before it is entered into. The contract may be a definite agreement to purchase or it may be a "contingent purchase contract" (ie a contract which is subject to conditions, for example it may be an option). However in either case the contract itself (or

a written memorandum of its terms if it is not in writing) must be available at the meeting itself. In the case of a public company the authority to enter into the contract must specify an expiry date for the contract to be entered into, which must be not more than 18 months later. The contract terms must show the names of the members holding shares to which the proposed purchase relates. Also the resolution must be passed by the requisite majority, without use of the votes attaching to the shares proposed to be purchased.

20.2 Redeemable shares

A company can now issue shares which are to be redeemed or are liable to be redeemed at the option of the company or the shareholders, provided it is authorised to do so by its articles. The standard articles contain such a power. However no redeemable shares may be issued at a time when there are no issued shares of the company which are not redeemable (ie there must be no possibility of the company having only redeemable shares).

Except in the case of private companies (see **20.3** below) redeemable shares may only be redeemed out of distributable profits of the company or out of the proceeds of a fresh issue of shares made for the purpose of the redemption.

20.3 Special provisions applying to private companies

In the case of private companies only, redeemable shares may be redeemed or shares of the company purchased out of capital provided the company's articles expressly permit such payments to be made out of capital (the standard articles do contain such a power). However in order to protect the interests of creditors, and indeed the shareholders, special procedures must be followed before any redemption or payment can be made out capital. These may be summarised as follows:

(a) The directors must make a statutory declaration that the company would be solvent following the proposed redemption or payment and that, having regard to the prospects and their intentions for the company, the company will be able to pay its debts as they fall due during the following year. The directors' declaration has to have an auditor's report annexed to it stating (*inter alia*) that the auditors are not aware of anything to indicate that the directors' opinion is unreasonable. As with all such declarations a director who makes it without reasonable grounds is guilty of an offence.

(b) The shareholders must pass a special resolution authorising the redemption or payment.
(c) The company must publicise its proposed payment out of capital before giving effect to it – the advertisement must appear in the Gazette (a government publication containing official notices) and the company must either notify every creditor or publish an advertisement in a national newspaper. A shareholder who does not consent or any creditor is allowed to apply to the court within five weeks of the resolution, and the court can make orders to protect the creditors or to deal with dissenting shareholders or to cancel the resolution.
(d) In making the redemption or payment the company must first use up its available profits before resorting to capital.

So far as directors are concerned, they also need to note that if they make a statutory declaration (as above) they can be personally liable for the debts of the company (up to the amount so paid) if the company goes into insolvent liquidation within 12 months unless the director concerned can show he had reasonable grounds for forming the opinion stated in the declaration. As with all such declarations, directors must therefore exercise great care when making them.

20.4 Other reductions of capital

Apart from the above permitted redemptions and purchases of the company's own shares, it is possible for a company to reduce its share capital by making an application to the court. However this is an entirely different procedure and it involves a court application.

20.5 Tax

Particularly in relation to the purchase of a company's own shares, the tax consequences need to be considered carefully.

CHAPTER 21

Transfer of shares

21.1 General

Shares in a company are freely transferable unless there is a clear provision in the articles which restricts the right to transfer the shares generally or in particular circumstances – see **21.3** below.

21.2 Form of transfer

Shares must be transferred by a written instrument of transfer (although the Companies Act 1989 paves the way for introducing paperless electronic transfers in due course). There is a standard statutory form of transfer which can be used. If the share is fully paid, then it is not necessary for the transferee to sign the transfer form.

The company must not register the share transfer unless it has been stamped with the appropriate stamp duty. Currently, stamp duty is at the rate of 0.5% of the purchase price paid.

21.3 Restrictions on transfer and pre-emption rights

What restrictions (if any) there are on the transfer of shares depends on the articles of association. (However shareholders' agreements may also contain restrictions on transfers of shares).

Public companies
(a) Public companies can have restrictions on transfer in their articles (as per private companies, see below) but usually they are fairly limited (such as in relation to partly paid shares or shares on which the company has a lien). In the case of companies whose shares are listed on the Stock Exchange, they are generally not permitted to have restrictions on transfers in their articles.

Private companies
(b) Private companies usually do have restrictions on transfers in their articles. These may be of two kinds:
    (i) *Pre-emption provisions*
        First of all, the articles may contain pre-emption provisions whereby any shareholder who wants to transfer his shares must first offer them for sale to existing shareholders or

possibly to the directors. No such article is included in the standard articles and the precise wording of any relevant article must be considered carefully because the provisions are almost always fairly complex and can vary widely in the way they operate. Sometimes transfers to existing members or relatives of existing members are exempted from pre-emption requirements. In principle any pre-emption provisions in a company's articles will be binding, though it may well be a matter of interpretation as to how far they extend.

(ii) *Discretion to refuse to register transfer*

The second restriction which private companies' articles often contain is a provision whereby the directors are given a discretion as to whether or not to register a share transfer. Again, such a provision is generally effective and if the directors refuse to register a share transfer that decision will be binding, unless it can be proved that the directors were acting in bad faith. If however, as is often the case, the article states that not only do the directors have a discretion but also that they do not have to give any reason for their refusal then, if they simply reject the transfer without any reason, it will be virtually impossible to prove there was any bad faith. If on the other hand the article states that the directors can only refuse to register a transfer on certain specified grounds, then the directors can probably be required to state their grounds and their decision would only be open to challenge if it did not fall within the permitted grounds under the articles.

If the directors decide to refuse to register a share transfer then this must normally be done within two months.

21.4 Share certificates

By statute companies must issue share certificates within two months after the date on which an effective share transfer is lodged for registration.

CHAPTER 22

Directors and shareholders

22.1 General duties to shareholders

Directors do not generally owe duties to individual shareholders: their duty is to act in the interests of the company as a whole, including its present shareholders as a group and, where appropriate, taking into account the interests of future shareholders as well.

Insofar as directors can be said to have duties to shareholders individually, their duties might be said to be:
(a) Not to mislead shareholders, if they are giving them advice.
(b) To act fairly and not to disregard the rights of minority shareholders (see **22.7** below).

22.2 Directors' dealings which require shareholder approval

In general, as mentioned in chapter 10, articles usually permit directors to deal freely with the company provided they disclose their interests at a board meeting. However, as mentioned elsewhere, certain dealings are prohibited (see chapters 11-12) and certain dealings, by statute, require prior shareholder approval, for example:
(a) Compensation for loss of office (see **11.5** above).
(b) Service contracts longer than five years (see **11.2** above).
(c) Substantial property transactions (see **11.4** above).

22.3 Other shareholder approval

Whilst management of the company's business is generally delegated to the directors under the articles, in certain cases the articles may contain provisions requiring particular matters to be approved by the shareholders. In addition there are certain matters which statute requires must be authorised or approved by shareholders, for example:
(a) Issue of shares (see **18.4** above).
(b) Purchase of company's own shares (see **20.1** and **20.3** above).

22.4 Circulars

When directors are convening a meeting of shareholders to propose resolutions for shareholder approval, they will generally send out a circular explaining the proposals.

Great care must be taken in preparing such circulars to ensure that they are fair. If the directors have an "interest" in the proposals being put forward, this must in particular be made clear. If the contents of a circular are misleading or fail to disclose a director's interest properly then shareholders may be able to get the resolution set aside, even if on the face of it the resolution was duly passed by the requisite majority. This is especially true in the case of matters in which the directors have an interest and if those interests are not fully and frankly disclosed.

In addition to the general legal position regarding circulars, there are specific statutory provisions. For example when directors are proposing to shareholders that a resolution should be passed to exclude the statutory pre-emption rights on share issues, then the directors may be criminally liable if they make any misleading, false or deceptive statement in their circular to shareholders (see **18.5** above). It is also a criminal offence generally for a director to make a false written statement or account to either members or creditors of a company, with a view to deceiving them.

Where directors do send a circular when convening a shareholders' meeting, there is nothing to prevent a body of shareholders who oppose the directors' proposals from themselves circulating shareholders expressing their contrary views, though obviously this would have to be done at the cost of the shareholders concerned (whereas directors have the advantage of being able to send their circulars at the cost of the company). Shareholders do however have a statutory right to require the company to circulate any statement of not more than 1,000 words with respect to any resolution proposed at a shareholders' meeting providing those shareholders constitute not less than 1/20th of the voting rights of the company or comprise not less than 100 members each having on average not less than £100 worth of paid up shares. However this statutory provision is not of great advantage since it limits the number of words which may be contained in the statement and it is still at the shareholders' expense unless the company otherwise resolves.

22.5 Prospectuses

If the directors have to take care about the wording of circulars which they send to shareholders then they more especially have to take care in relation to the wording of prospectus type documents.

Where a company is listed on the Stock Exchange it has to submit listing particulars containing information about the company and its shares, and if the company's shares are to be listed on an exchange other than the Stock Exchange then a prospectus will have to be approved by that exchange. If a company is not listed on the Stock Exchange then it cannot publicly offer its shares unless a prospectus has been registered at Companies House. It is not possible to go into detail on the various requirements relating to listing particulars and propectuses, but only to deal with the general principles. For this purpose listing particulars will be treated as prospectuses, since similar provisions apply to both.

There is a statutory duty to include in prospectuses all such information as investors and their professional advisers would reasonably require and reasonably expect to find for the purposes of making an informed assessment of the assets and liabilities, financial position, profits and losses and prospects of the company issuing the securities, and the rights attaching to those securities.

A prospectus must be delivered for registration to the Registrar of Companies on or before the date it is published otherwise any person (which includes a director) who is knowingly a party to the publication is guilty of an offence.

In addition those responsible for any prospectus (which includes the directors) may be liable to pay compensation to any person who acquires any of the securities in question and suffers loss in respect of them as a result of any untrue or misleading statement or the omission of any matters required to be included. However a director will have a defence to this liability if he satisfies the court that at the time the prospectus was submitted he reasonably believed, having made such enquiries (if any) as were reasonable, that the statement was true and not misleading (or that the matter omitted which caused the loss was properly omitted) and that he continued in that belief up until the time when the securities were acquired or that they were acquired before it was reasonably practicable to bring a correction to the attention of persons likely to acquire the securities or that before the securities were acquired he had taken all such steps as were reasonable for him to take to secure that a correction was brought to the attention of those persons.

Also in the case of a director he would not be liable for any statement made by an expert which is included in the prospectus with the expert's consent if at the relevant time the director believed on reasonable grounds that the person was competent to make the statement.

It will be seen from the above that directors who issue prospectuses have a very considerable duty to ensure that all relevant information is included in the prospectus and that every statement contained in the prospectus is very carefully checked. For this reason it is usual to have a specific board meeting in which the prospectus is gone through virtually word for word and the source of belief for a particular statement is noted and carefully considered. The persons liable for a prospectus are all persons who are named in the prospectus as directors or as having agreed to become directors unless the prospectus is issued without a person's knowledge or his consent and on becoming aware of it he forthwith gives reasonable public notice that it was delivered without his knowledge or consent. In practice the details of the prospectus are often delegated to a committee of the board, but since every director is personally responsible it is important that they should all keep up to date with the current draft of the prospectus and should check it carefully.

22.6 Takeovers

There is no general statutory provision about how takeovers must be effected. However the City Code on Takeovers and Mergers, which basically is intended to apply to listed companies and other public companies prescribes that when one company proposes to make a takeover offer for another company then the offer should first be put to the board of the target company. The directors of the target company are then obliged to take competent independent advice on the offer and then to make their recommendations to shareholders together with details of that advice. In carrying out this function directors have a duty to act in their capacity as directors and without regard to their own personal shareholdings, ie they should advise their shareholders fairly.

In putting forward its offer the acquiring company will have to comply with various statutory and other requirements. So far as the target company is concerned, the directors can send a circular to their shareholders with their recommendations.

Another important aspect of the Code is that directors must not try and frustrate the takeover by artificial means.

In connection with a takeover or the transfer of the whole or any part of the property of the company, it is not lawful for any payment to be made to any director by way of compensation for loss of office or in connection with his retirement from office unless particulars of the proposed payment have been disclosed to shareholders and the proposal approved by the company. It is not only an offence but also the director will not be entitled to keep any such payment if it has not been approved (see 11.5 above).

22.7 Minority rights

It is a general rule of company law that if some wrong is done to a company (eg a breach by a director of his duties) the proper plaintiff is the company itself, not its shareholders, and secondly that the courts will not generally interfere with the internal management of a company which is acting within its powers. Normally therefore it is very difficult for an individual shareholder to bring an action in relation to the company's affairs unless the majority of shareholders are in agreement.

However, there are certain exceptions to this rule. First of all, an individual shareholder can complain if a transaction is being entered into which is illegal or beyond the powers of the company or if a special or extraordinary resolution of the company is required to decide the matter and such a resolution has not been passed. A further exception is that the majority shareholders cannot take away a shareholder's personal rights (eg his right to vote) and therefore an individual shareholder can sue in such circumstances. A third category of exception is where the action amounts to a "fraud on the minority" and the wrongdoers are in control of the company (ie where the majority will not take effective action because it is they who have committed the wrong). The type of matters which might be covered by this are expropriation of company property for the benefit of the majority or fraudulent action by directors. However if the matter does not amount to a fraud (eg if it is merely negligence on the part of the directors) then the majority of shareholders can usually ratify that action (see 7.5 above) and it would not constitute a fraud on the minority.

In addition to the above, there are various statutory provisions which give rights to minority shareholders:

(a) A shareholder can apply to the court to wind-up the company on the grounds that it is just and equitable to do so. The type of situation where this may apply is if shareholders have jointly formed a company with the intention that each would remain directors and take part in its management, but one of them is voted off the board by the others. This obviously is a fairly severe remedy and in practice it is more likely to be dealt with nowadays under the more recent statutory provision referred to in (b) below.

(b) A shareholder may apply to the court on the grounds that the company's affairs are being or have been conducted in a manner which is "unfairly prejudicial" to the interests of all or some of the members (or that any actual or proposed act or omission of the company would be prejudicial). The court has a very wide discretion as to what order to make if unfair prejudice is proved. The order can include permitting a shareholder to take proceedings on behalf of the company, providing for a member's shares to be bought out by the company or by other members, or regulating the company's affairs for the future. The type of matter complained of could include total failure to pay dividends, particularly if the majority of shareholders are directors and are taking most of the profits out by way of directors' remuneration.

(c) Apart from the above there are several other statutory provisions whereby a certain number of the shareholders have the right to apply to the court if they object to certain procedural matters. For example, even where a special resolution has been passed to alter a company's objects, the holders of 15% of the shares who disagree can apply to the court to cancel the alteration. Similarly, holders of 15% of a class of shares can apply to the court to cancel a proposed variation of their class rights.

In carrying out their duties, directors should always consider the position of minority shareholders and the fact that they may have rights to complain if they are dealt with in a prejudicial manner.

CHAPTER 23

Shareholders' meetings

23.1 Annual general meeting

The most important shareholders' meeting is the annual general meeting and indeed for many companies it will often be the only shareholders' meeting during the year.

Directors are required to arrange for the company to have an annual general meeting of shareholders once in each calendar year (but see **24.5** below regarding the recently introduced exemption in the case of private companies). The first annual general meeting must be held within 18 months of the company's incorporation, and thereafter not more than 15 months must elapse between each annual general meeting. Not less than 21 days' clear notice (excluding the date of sending out the notice and the date of the meeting) must be given to all shareholders of the date and place of the meeting and the general business to be transacted at the meeting.

The meeting can be called on shorter notice provided all the members entitled to attend and vote at the meeting give their consent to this. In practice this provision is only useful to small private companies where there are few shareholders, or in the case of subsidiary companies, where the parent company and its nominee shareholder can readily give their consent.

The usual business to be transacted at an annual general meeting is the following:

1 Receipt of the audited accounts.
2 Declaration of a dividend.
3 Election of directors.
4 Re-appointment of auditors.

The annual general meeting is a shareholders' meeting like any other shareholders' meeting and therefore any other matters (eg special resolutions) can be included as part of the business to be dealt with. Sometimes companies prefer, if there is to be a special resolution or other special business, that it should be held at an extraordinary general meeting to take place immediately after the annual general meeting. This is perfectly in order, but there is no technical reason why the resolutions should not be dealt with at the annual general meeting itself.

It may sometimes happen that the audited accounts of a company are not available for some reason (eg because of a change of the accounting reference date) by the time within which the annual general meeting has to be held. In such a case the annual general meeting should be held without the audited accounts and the audited accounts can be approved at a subsequent extraordinary general meeting or at an adjournment of the annual general meeting.

23.2 Annual return: filing of audited accounts

Probably the most important documents which a company has to file at the Companies Registry are the annual return form and the audited accounts of the company. Most company prosecutions relate to a failure to file annual returns and annual accounts.

Annual return
(a) The annual return has to be completed on the prescribed form. Under the Companies Act 1989 the annual return form must be completed and delivered to the Registrar of Companies (together with the appropriate registration fee, currently £20) within 28 days of the company's return date. A company's return date is the anniversary of the company's incorporation or 12 months from the date of the last annual return.

Audited accounts
(b) The audited accounts have to be sent to the Registrar of Companies. It is common for the audited accounts to be filed at the Companies Registry at the same time as the annual return form, but they can be filed separately. The time limit for filing the audited accounts is within 10 months after the end of the accounting reference period in the case of private companies and seven months in the case of public companies. Under the Companies Act 1989 the file copy of the company's accounts will need to be signed by only one director on behalf of the board.

23.3 Extraordinary general meetings

Any general meeting of shareholders, other than the annual general meeting, is called an extraordinary general meeting. Whether any extraordinary general meetings will be required by a company in any year will depend entirely on what matters may require shareholder approval, ie matters which statute or the articles require to be decided on by the shareholders.

An extraordinary general meeting must be held on 14 clear days' notice (or 21 if a special resolution is proposed), but if a majority of shareholders holding at least 95% of votes agree, shorter notice is permitted. (This contrasts with an annual general meeting, where all shareholders must agree if notice is shortened or dispensed with.) (The figure of 95% may be reduced to 90% if a private company has passed an elective resolution – see **24.5** below.)

23.4 Class meetings

Where a company's share capital is divided into different classes of shares, eg preference shares and ordinary shares, it is sometimes desired to alter the rights attaching to the shares, and this can only be done with the requisite authority of the holders of the particular class of shares affected. Statute and the articles of association generally permit class rights to be varied provided that the holders of three-quarters in nominal value of the issued shares of that class consent in writing to the variation or an extraordinary resolution is passed at a separate general meeting of the holders of that class of shares. There will therefore be occasions when not only are there extraordinary general meetings of the company but there are also separate meetings of holders of particular classes of shares. At a class meeting only shareholders of that class should be present and not, for example, other shareholders waiting for an extraordinary general meeting which follows.

A dissenting minority also has a right to apply to the court in certain circumstances to prevent a variation of their rights.

Class rights are in general only regarded as varied where there is a direct alteration to the rights of that particular class (for example altering the rate of fixed dividend, the voting rights or other specific rights actually attached to the shares). There is not usually a variation of class rights by implication (although there are exceptions to this in extreme cases). For example, issuing a new class of shares will not generally be regarded as of itself varying the class rights of other existing shares, even though, for example, the practical effect on voting may be significant. However the articles may expressly provide that certain matters are deemed to be a variation of class rights, in which case the provisions of the articles would obviously govern the situation.

23.5 Calling shareholders' meetings

The directors manage the company and normally it is the directors who convene shareholders' meetings because there are matters or transactions or resolutions which need to be approved or passed by shareholders in order to implement them. To convene a shareholders' meeting the directors must first decide by resolution of the board that there should be a shareholders' meeting.

However shareholders have the right to convene shareholders' meetings in certain circumstances. Shareholders can require shareholders' meetings to be held provided those requisitioning the meeting represent at least 10% of the total voting rights of the company by value. On receiving such a requisition the directors must within 21 days proceed to convene a meeting, and if they do not do so then the requisitioners can proceed to call the meeting and recover the costs from the company. The company can in turn recover the costs out of fees or other remuneration which may become payable to the directors who are in default.

In addition, the same number of shareholders (or alternatively not less than 100 shareholders holding shares on which, on average, at least £100 has been paid up) are entitled to require that a resolution should be put at the next annual general meeting and that a statement from them of not more than 1,000 words regarding such proposed resolution or business is also circulated.

Apart from the above, there is no express requirement for the directors to call extraordinary general meetings at any time except that in the case of a public company the directors are under a duty to call an extraordinary general meeting within 56 days of becoming aware of the situation if net assets fall to 50% or less of called up share capital – ie if more than 50% of the paid up share capital has been lost. In such a case there is however no statutory action which a company must take – it must simply consider the position, and no doubt the directors are intended to recommend some proposal.

23.6 Conduct of meetings

The conduct of meetings depends principally on what the articles say, which normally will be as follows.

Before there can be an effective meeting, there has to be a quorum present. In relation to general meetings the quorum will be set down in the articles of association but will normally be two members present in person or by proxy. In the case of class meetings it may be a requirement under the articles (and by statute) that the quorum holds a minimum number of shares of the particular class.

The articles generally provide that the chairman of the board is to act as chairman at a general meeting, but if he is not willing to act or is not present within 15 minutes, then the directors may appoint another director to act in his place, failing which the shareholders present may elect one of their number to act as chairman.

Any resolution put to the meeting is to be decided on a show of hands unless before, or on the declaration of the result of the show of hands, a poll is demanded by the chairman or by two members having the right to vote, or by a member or members representing not less than one-tenth of the total voting rights. A person acting as proxy can be counted as a person demanding a poll.

If there is an equality of votes, then the chairman generally has a casting vote under the articles (though in the case of a small evenly balanced company, this provision may have been deleted in order to maintain equality).

23.7 Proxies

When calling a general meeting of shareholders, directors must ensure that there appears, in the notice of meeting (with reasonable prominence) a statement that a member entitled to attend and vote at the meeting is entitled to appoint a proxy, who need not himself be a shareholder. Also, if directors send out proxy forms, then they must send them to all members and not simply to those who they feel would be sympathetic to the resolution. Proxy forms cannot be required to be lodged with the company earlier than 48 hours before the meeting at which they are to be used. The standard articles of association set out a possible form of proxy but generally permit the form of proxy to be in any usual form or other form which the directors approve.

A proxy cannot vote on a show of hands, but can demand that a vote is taken by a poll instead. Also, in a public company, a proxy has no right to speak at a meeting.

Where a company is a member of another company, it is entitled to appoint a representative by resolution of its board and such a representative is treated as if he was the company present in person, ie he is not a proxy.

23.8 Adjournments

The chairman may, with the consent of a meeting at which a quorum is present, and shall if so directed by the meeting, adjourn the meeting from time to time, but no meeting may be transacted at the adjourned meeting other than the business to have been dealt with at the original meeting.

If the meeting is adjourned then the time and place for the adjourned meeting is decided. If the adjournment is for 14 days or more, then at least seven clear days' notice must be given specifying the time and place of the adjourned meeting and the general nature of the business to be transacted. On any shorter adjournment it is not necessary to give any further notice to members.

Where a resolution is passed at an adjourned meeting, then it is regarded as passed on the date of the adjourned meeting (and not any earlier date).

There are various reasons why it may be necessary to adjourn the meeting. One particular instance where an adjournment is compulsory is where a quorum is not present within half an hour from the time appointed for the meeting or if during the meeting a quorum ceases to be present. In such cases the meeting automatically stands adjourned to the same day the next week at the same time and place or to such time and place as the directors may determine.

23.9 Minutes of meetings

A company must keep minutes of its shareholders' meetings, and such minutes, if signed by the chairman of the meeting or the next succeeding meeting, are evidence of the proceedings, and until the contrary is proved, the meeting is deemed to have been duly held.

CHAPTER 24

Shareholders' resolutions

24.1 Types of resolutions

Resolutions which are put to shareholders may be ordinary resolutions, special resolutions, extraordinary resolutions or elective resolutions – the type of resolution required for any matter is determined by statute and by the articles of association.

(a) *A special resolution* is a resolution which has been passed by a majority of not less than three-quarters of the votes cast. But to be effective not less than 21 days' notice must have been given of the meeting and of the special resolution to be proposed (unless notice is waived by a majority of shareholders who hold at least 95% of the voting shares by nominal value).

(b) *An extraordinary resolution* is a resolution passed by a majority of not less than three-quarters of the votes cast but in that case not less than 14 days' notice must have been given of the meeting and of the extraordinary resolution to be proposed. In practice extraordinary resolutions are only used rarely, where required by statute in relation to certain matters relating to the winding up of a company. Otherwise, a special resolution is used where something more than an ordinary resolution is required.

(c) *An ordinary resolution* is one which is passed by a simple majority (over 50%) of votes cast. Not less than 14 days' notice must have been given convening the general meeting at which the resolution is to be passed.

(d) *An elective resolution* is a new type of resolution applying to private companies which has been introduced by the Companies Act 1989. It has to be agreed to by all members entitled to vote. Twenty-one days' notice of a meeting to pass an elective resolution must be given.

Typical examples of matters requiring shareholders' approval, and the types of resolution required by statute or by normal articles of association are as follows:

(a) Change of company's name (special resolution).
(b) Increase of authorised share capital and authorising directors to issue shares (ordinary resolution).
(c) Alteration of company's objects clause or articles of association (special resolution).
(d) Permitting shares to be issued otherwise than proportionally to existing shareholders (special resolution).
(e) Alteration of class rights attaching to shares (special resolution and also class meeting required).
(f) Reduction of share capital (special resolution – court approval may also be required).
(g) Purchase by private company of own shares (special resolution).
(h) Removal of director (ordinary resolution)
(i) Approval of ex-gratia compensation to retiring director (ordinary resolution).
(j) Ratification of directors' transactions (normally ordinary resolution).
(k) Revoking an elective resolution by private company (ordinary resolution).

24.2 Amendments to resolutions

At a shareholders' meeting, amendments can be made to ordinary resolutions provided they are within the scope of the business covered by the resolution, but in the case of extraordinary resolutions and special resolutions, only very limited amendments may be made (eg clerical errors).

24.3 Written resolutions

Articles of a company can permit resolutions of shareholders to be in the form of written resolutions signed by or on behalf of all the shareholders (instead of a meeting being held). The standard articles expressly permit such written resolutions, and state that such resolutions shall be as effective as if they had been passed at a general meeting. The standard articles also state that such resolutions may be in the form of several written and signed documents (eg each member could sign a copy rather than having all the members sign the same document). The wording of the articles needs to be checked however.

The articles of any company, whether public or private, may provide for written resolutions, but it is only likely to be practical for smaller private companies with few members to proceed by way of written resolution. Also, if every member does not agree to the resolution, one can only proceed by calling a meeting and obtaining the requisite majority for passing the resolution.

Although the standard articles in respect of written resolutions (and indeed most companies' articles have similar provisions) permit written resolutions generally and envisage that an ordinary, special or extraordinary resolution (as the case may require) may be passed in this way, there have been some doubts as to whether certain limited types of resolution can be passed in this way in view of the fact that the statutes lay down in some cases certain procedures which must be followed before certain specific resolutions can be passed. For example the procedures for removing an auditor or a director permit the auditor or director to make representations before being removed (see **16.5** above and **26.4** below) and see also the specific resolutions set out in **24.4** (a) (iii) below. The position is not entirely clear, but it may be that in respect of the removal of directors and auditors a meeting is technically required, and that in the case of the items listed in section **24.4** (a) (iii) below a meeting is also required technically, unless the statutory procedure in **24.4** below is followed.

24.4 Statutory written resolutions (private companies)

The Companies Act 1989 is introducing a new statutory procedure for private companies (not public companies) to pass written resolutions. The statutory procedure can apply to any form of resolution of shareholders (or class of shareholders) including the new elective resolutions referred to in **24.5** below. The general procedure is similar to the procedure for passing resolutions under the standard articles (see **24.3** above) and requires the signature by or on behalf of all shareholders entitled to vote on the issue. There are, however, certain procedural aspects which need to be noted, and also certain exceptions. This statutory procedure for written resolutions is only likely to be beneficial if the company's articles contain no provision for written resolutions or in cases (as in **24.4** (a) (iii)) where a written resolution under the articles may not be legally effective.

Procedural aspects
- (a) (i) A copy of any proposed written resolution must first be sent to the company's auditors, and the auditors are entitled within seven days of receipt to give notice to the company stating that in their opinion the resolution should be considered by the company in general meeting (or by a class meeting). A written resolution does not have effect unless the auditors notify the company that the resolution does not

concern them as auditors or need not be considered by the company in general meeting or unless the seven day period referred to has expired.

(ii) Where a written resolution is agreed to as above a record of the resolution (and of the signatures) is to be entered in a book in the same way as minutes of a general meeting, and any such record if signed by a director or the secretary is evidence of the proceedings and compliance with the requirements, unless the contrary is proved.

(iii) Where the Companies Acts require certain documents to be circulated to members or to be available for members or other specific requirements to be dealt with before certain resolutions are passed, then the relevant documents must be provided to all members at or before they sign the resolution. The types of resolution referred to are:
(1) disapplication of pre-emption rights – see **18.5** above;
(2) financial assistance for purchase of company's own shares – see **19.3** above;
(3) authority for off-market purchase or contingent purchase contract of company's own shares – see **20.1(b)** above;
(4) approval for payment out of capital – see **20.3** above;
(5) approval of director's service contract – see **11.2(b)** above;
(6) funding of director's expenditure in performing his duties – see **11.3(b)(ii)** above.

Exceptions
(b) It is not possible for a statutory written resolution to deal with the following types of resolution:
(i) removal of auditors – see **16.5** above;
(ii) removal of a director – see **26.4** above.
In such cases a meeting would have to be held.

24.5 Elective resolutions (private companies)

The Companies Act 1989 is introducing a new type of resolution applicable only to private companies and called an "elective resolution". As in the case of a special resolution, at least 21 days' notice in writing must be given of a meeting at which it is proposed to pass an elective resolution, and the resolution must be agreed to at the meeting, in person or by proxy, by all the members entitled to attend and vote at the meeting. Alternatively, an elective resolution can be passed by unanimous written resolution.

The general idea of an elective resolution is that private companies can, by passing an elective resolution, adopt somewhat more simplified procedures, if so desired. Once an elective resolution has been passed, the company may, by ordinary resolution, at any time revoke the elective resolution. Copies of elective resolutions and resolutions revoking them, have to be filed at the Companies Registry within 14 days.

Elective resolutions can be passed by private companies for the following purposes:
  (a) to grant directors power to issue shares for more than five years or indefinitely – see **18.4** above;
  (b) to elect to dispense with the laying of accounts and reports before a general meeting of shareholders – see **16.4** above;
  (c) to elect to dispense with the holding of an annual general meeting – see **23.1** above;
  (d) to elect that general meetings can be held on shorter notice than would otherwise be required with the consent of the holders of 90% of the shares or more (rather than 95%) (see **23.3**);
  (e) to elect to dispense with the appointment of auditors annually (ie so that the auditors would simply continue in office unless or until a resolution was passed to remove them – see **16.5** above);

Regulations may be made under the Act by which other matters can be dealt with by elective resolution.

CHAPTER 25

Litigation

25.1 Outline of proceedings

In normal civil proceedings in the High Court, when claims are made for breach of contract and the like, the usual course is as follows. The plaintiff issues a writ which may include a detailed statement of the claim or may state the claim in general terms.

The defendant must file an acknowledgement of service within 14 days, failing which the plaintiff may obtain judgment in default.

Once the defendant has indicated in the acknowledgement of service that he intends to defend the proceedings, the parties serve on each other what are known as "pleadings", in which the plaintiff and defendant indicate in written form, the nature of their claim and defence (and possibly counterclaim). These are designed to clarify what the issues are between the parties, and to identify what the real areas of disputes are.

After the parties have narrowed down the issues in this way, the parties have to serve on each other lists of documents (see **25.4** below).

Following that and any other procedural aspects (which may take many months), there will then be a trial before a judge.

If at the outset a plaintiff considers that there is no reasonable defence to his claim, then it is possible for him to apply for summary judgment in his favour on those grounds. This is done on the basis of written affidavits and a hearing without witnesses being present.

25.2 Importance of written records

The vast majority of court cases are settled before they reach a hearing. There are of course a great many reasons for this and often the time and costs of proceedings are relevant factors. However in quite a few cases the absence of written records can be a significant factor. Particularly in detailed matters it is surprising how quickly things can be forgotten with the result that a failure to confirm something in writing or in a note can make it much more difficult to prove at a later date.

25.3 "Without prejudice" and "subject to contract"

Both these expressions have their uses in connection with legal proceedings or the threat of legal proceedings, and may help to avoid them altogether. It is important therefore to appreciate the meaning of the expressions:

"Without prejudice"
(a) It is part of public policy to encourage the settlement of disputes. However, parties would not want to be seen to be willing to resolve their differences if the other party could later say in court that this indicated that they accepted liability for the claim. However if the offer is made in a letter, or as part of a discussion, which is expressed to be "without prejudice" then the contents of that letter or discussion cannot be used as evidence in the proceedings. It is therefore of great practical advantage to be able to make "without prejudice" offers. "Without prejudice" is effectively shorthand for "without prejudice to my case if we fail to reach a settlement". However there are nonetheless various points to be borne in mind:

(i) It is the offer itself which cannot be used in evidence. If the letter goes beyond mere argument and proposals for settlement but goes on to make some kind of admission (eg that the reason the person cannot make any greater offer is that he is unable to pay his debts), then that admission may be used in evidence. This is just one example to illustrate that, despite the benefits of "without prejudice" correspondence, one does have to be a little careful about what is said.

(ii) If the other party accepts the offer then the agreement becomes completely "open" and legally binding.

(iii) If a party wants to make a "without prejudice" offer to dispose of the matter, then it is usually advisable to have two separate letters, the first letter an open letter stating his case and then a separate "without prejudice" letter containing the offer. If this is not done then there will be no "open" letter (ie which can be referred to in evidence) since neither party can refer to its own "without prejudice" letters without the consent of the other party.

"Subject to contract"
(b) The purpose of this expression is to show that it is not intended that a particular proposal being made should, if accepted, amount to an immediate binding contract. The words mean that the proposals are subject to a condition that before a binding contract exists, there first must be a formal agreement signed by the parties. In rare circumstances the courts have not given effect to this meaning but generally speaking if these words are used, they will

be effective to prevent a binding contract coming into existence at that stage.

The use of these words can therefore be helpful to prevent an argument as to whether a binding contract was intended to come into effect as a result of an exchange of correspondence. It can also be useful in connection with legal proceedings where the parties are trying to reach a settlement in principle (but do not want to be committed until all the details have been discussed and agreed).

25.4 Discovery

If legal proceedings look likely on any matter, it is worth bearing in mind that in most civil proceedings there is automatic "discovery" of documents. This means that each party to a dispute has to make a list disclosing all the documents in his possession, custody or power relating to the dispute (letters, correspondence, tape recordings or anything else which can be converted into written form), and the originals of all these documents have to be disclosed to the other party (and copies provided, if requested). This includes documents which a party has which are prejudicial to his own case, because public policy demands that the courts get at the truth of the matter.

Certain documents, however, are "privileged" from inspection and do not need to be disclosed, principally those relating to the taking and obtaining of legal advice and preparing for litigation (eg witness statements, discussions with experts, etc).

It is important to appreciate that discovery is very wide ranging, and one has to disclose even internal documents and notes, diary entries and indeed anything at all in written form, unless it is "privileged". Particularly where there is some continuing element involved in the dispute, it is important to appreciate that even documents created after the start of proceedings are subject to discovery, unless they fall within the category of privileged documents.

Where any dispute looks imminent, it is important to ensure that no original documents relating to the dispute are destroyed because the worst possible interpretation may be put on this in any subsequent proceedings. Even where the company has a procedure for microfilming documents, it is important not to destory the original and any documents relating to a potential dispute should be kept separate. It also needs to be borne in mind that it is an offence for an officer of a company to destroy or falsify any original documents unless there is no intention to defeat the law or conceal the truth about the company's affairs.

25.5 Action to take

In the High Court a company can only conduct proceedings through solicitors. In the county court, while a company can commence or carry on proceedings itself, it is not permitted to appear at hearings in court (through a director or employee), unless the court so permits. Generally therefore it is important that a company should obtain legal advice at the earliest opportunity. Whether as a plaintiff or defendant, there are many orders and applications which can be made in court proceedings on very short notice, particularly where rights may be prejudiced or documents or other evidence may cease to be available.

The costs of litigation are often high and there are procedures whereby a defendant can make offers (eg by paying the money into court) which can lessen the risk of having to pay all the plaintiff's costs if the plaintiff refuses an offer which later proves to be greater than what the court awards. Such procedures can facilitate a settlement in appropriate cases.

25.6 Limitation of actions

Proceedings must normally be commenced within six years from the date on which the cause of action accrued (three years in the case of personal injury). However in the case of contractual claims where the contract is under seal, the limitation period is 12 years from the date on which the cause of action accrued.

CHAPTER 26

Ceasing to be a director

26.1 Resignation

A director may at any time resign as a director of the company and articles generally require no formality other than notice to the company. If a director has a service contract with the company in his capacity as an executive director then immediate resignation may be a breach of that agreement. However the resignation itself will be effective.

26.2 Retirement by rotation

The standard articles provide that at the first annual general meeting all the directors shall retire from office and at every subsequent annual general meeting one third of the directors (or the nearest number to one third) shall retire by rotation. The directors who are to retire by rotation are those who have been longest in office since their last appointment or re-appointment, but as between persons whose length in office is the same, this is determined by lot, unless they otherwise agree. However, managing directors and other executive directors are not required to retire by rotation. In the case of small private companies particularly, these articles are often deleted.

A director retiring by rotation is eligible for re-election and indeed the articles usually provide that if he is willing to continue to act and no one is appointed in his place, then he is deemed to be re-elected (unless a resolution to re-appoint him has been defeated).

Where the directors appoint a new director in the course of the year, either to fill a casual vacancy or as an additional director, then the articles normally provide that he retires at the next annual general meeting (in addition to the other directors retiring by rotation).

26.3 Disqualification

Articles normally provide for a director to vacate his office automatically if certain circumstances arise. For example the standard articles state that a director vacates office automatically if he becomes prohibited from being a director (see **15.10** above) or if he becomes bankrupt or if he becomes subject to the mental health statutes.

Also articles generally provide that if a director is absent for more than six consecutive months, without the permission of the directors, from meetings of directors held during that period then he will cease to be a director if the other directors pass a resolution to that effect.

26.4 Removal

Statute provides that, notwithstanding anything in the articles or in any agreement, the company may always remove a director from office by a shareholders' ordinary resolution at any time. A person who intends to propose such a resolution must give the company not less than 28 days' notice. The company must then notify the director concerned and he is entitled to require the company to circulate to members his representations regarding his removal (provided they are not defamatory), and he is entitled to be heard at the meeting at which his removal is proposed. The right to remove a director is subject to any claim which he has for compensation or damages.

Articles may provide additional means whereby directors may be removed from office, for example by extraordinary resolution of the company. However unless the articles expressly give them the power, the directors themselves have no power to remove a director from office by a board resolution – the standard articles only give the board this power where the director concerned has been absent from board meetings for six months without permission.

26.5 Dismissal of an executive director

The legal distinction between being employed in an executive capacity and holding office as a director means that if an executive director is dismissed by his company (ie his employment is terminated), whether for incompetence or misconduct or whatever, it does not automatically follow that he ceases to hold office as a director. This can obviously be inconvenient. For this reason sometimes an executive director's service contract includes a provision requiring him to resign from office if his employment is terminated for any reason, together with an irrevocable authorisation for someone else to sign a resignation letter on his behalf if he refuses to do so at the time. Otherwise it will be necessary to go through the procedures described in **26.4** above.

26.6 Directors' rights on removal from office: compensation

If a director is removed from office, then he may have rights against the company. If he is purely a non-executive director, then he would normally have no rights. If however he performs an executive function within the company and has a service agreement or employment contract with the company then his removal from office may be a breach of that contract for which he would be entitled to compensation in the same way as any other employee who is wrongfully or unfairly dismissed.

Where a director has a service contract providing for a period of notice and the company terminates the contract without proper notice, then (unless he is himself in the wrong) the director has a claim for compensation. However like any employee, he is under a duty to mitigate his loss by seeking alternative employment, and from a legal point of view he is, strictly speaking, only entitled to recover his net loss, which in most cases will amount to the difference between the remuneration he would have obtained during his period of notice with the company and any remuneration actually received from other employment.

Under present tax rules any compensation paid up to £30,000 is exempt from tax, and the balance is subject to income tax. Any payment made by the company is usually deductible for corporation tax purposes, but it may be disallowed if the termination coincides with the director selling his shares in the company or if it is considered excessive.

If a service agreement or any other agreement actually provides for a specified sum to be paid on termination instead of notice, then the whole amount may be liable to taxation as ordinary remuneration in view of the fact that it has been expressly agreed in advance. If the amount paid exceeds the amount properly due under the service agreement, then the amount has to be approved by an ordinary resolution of the shareholders (see **11.5** above).

Where it is intended that a minority shareholder is to be entitled as of right to remain a director the articles sometimes give that director's shares extra votes on any resolution for his removal, giving him an absolute majority on that issue. This will generally be effective. In the absence of such express provision, if the company was established as a kind of partnership between the removed director and other persons on the basis that each was to participate in the management of the company, then the removal of that director may lead to an application by the director to the court either for the company to be wound up or for the court to provide some other remedy such as the director's shares being bought out.

26.7 Formalities

When a person ceases to be a director then he should ensure that Companies Registry is notified within 14 days and that any other appropriate persons are similarly notified, eg the company's bank, and if the company is in a regulated business, then any of the appropriate regulatory authorities also need to be notified. The register of directors will also need to be brought up to date.

Also, if the director has given any personal guarantees he should consider what steps (if any) can be taken to bring his liability to an end.

26.8 Activities prior to leaving

A director needs to bear in mind that, like any other employee, until such time as he leaves the company, his duties are to the company. He should not therefore be trying to take away the company's business or persuade employees to leave the company with him and start another business since until the time he actually leaves this would constitute a breach of his duties to the company.

26.9 Activities after leaving

As regards confidential information which he has obtained while a director of the company, the director, like any other employee, is under a duty to continue to treat that information as confidential after his directorship has terminated.

After he has left the company, a director is free to compete with the company in the normal way provided he does not use the company's trade secrets or similar confidential information of the company and provided also that he is not subject to any enforceable restrictive covenant contained in his contract of employment.

Executive directors are however often subject to restrictive covenants in their employment contracts restricting their activities after they have left. Typically, these may include restrictions on being engaged or interested in a competing business or soliciting the company's customers, suppliers or employees. Because these restrict potential trade and competition, and limit a director's freedom to use his skills and experience to earn a living, as a matter of public policy these types of clauses will only be enforced by the courts if they protect a legitimate interest of the company and are reasonable in all the circumstances – if they are too wide or last too long they will be unenforceable.

It is difficult to say with certainty what provisions will, or will not, be enforceable because so much depends on the circumstances of each particular case. Companies should seek expert advice when including such clauses in service contracts, and directors should seek expert advice before agreeing to such provisions.

CHAPTER 27

Particular companies and provisions

27.1 Listed companies and their subsidiaries

All the provisions mentioned already apply to companies whose shares are listed on the Stock Exchange.

However as listed companies involve a public market for the shares in the company (with any person being able to buy or sell shares on the Stock Exchange) additional requirements and duties are imposed by the Stock Exchange. These are aimed particularly at making sure there is a fair market in the shares and that information is promptly made available to investors. Obviously, therefore, it is essential that directors of listed companies familiarise themselves with the requirements.

Examples of some of these requirements are as follows:

(a) There is a general requirement that all information that may be material to investors should be promptly notified to the Stock Exchange. Also, where proposed developments are under discussion, directors must ensure that there is strict security until such time as an announcement can be made.

(b) Dates fixed for board meetings at which declarations of dividends will be decided or where half-yearly or yearly accounts will be approved, must be notified in advance.

(c) A listed company must prepare half-yearly accounts.

(d) Draft circulars and notices to shareholders must be submitted in advance to the Stock Exchange. In addition there are certain extra matters which must be included in circulars, eg for companies proposing to increase their authorised share capital, directors must state in the circular whether they have any present intention to issue any of the new shares.

(e) Unless shareholders otherwise permit, a company must obtain the consent of its shareholders before any major subsidiary of the company issues shares for cash which would dilute the company's interest.

(f) Changes of directors and senior executives must be notified immediately to the Stock Exchange.

(g) The company must adopt rules equivalent to the Model Code for directors' dealings in the company's own shares (see **12.3** above).

(h) A point which also needs to be borne in mind not only by directors of listed companies but also by directors of subsidiaries of listed companies is that they are themselves regarded as what the Stock Exchange rules call "Class 4 parties". "Class 4 parties" mean directors or substantial shareholders (or their associates). The Stock Exchange has various requirements whereby transactions between the company (or the subsidiary) and one of the directors of the company (or the subsidiary) must be notified or approved by shareholders. The usual types of transaction are any sale or purchase of assets by such a person or any issue of new shares for cash to such a person or certain loan transactions. If the transaction is a small transaction in relation to the size of the company then it will usually be possible to obtain dispensation from the Stock Exchange from circularising members provided the transaction can be shown to be at market value.

27.2 Regulated companies

There are a large number of companies nowadays which are regulated in their activities under various statutes, particularly in the financial sector. The regulation may be the responsibility of the Department of Trade or of other regulatory bodies. If a person is accepting a directorship in a company operating in such areas then he must obviously try and familiarise himself with the regulations which apply. Some examples of companies which are regulated in this way are banks, insurance companies and brokers, investment managers, share dealers, companies involved in consumer credit etc.

Apart from being familiar with the general regulations affecting the business, directors need to be sure that they or someone within the company is fully aware of what matters need to be approved in advance by the regulatory body and what matters need to be notified to them. For example before directors can approve a shareholder acquiring a controlling interest (usually defined as 15%) in such a company it is often necessary for the company to obtain the prior approval of the regulatory body. Likewise it is often necessary in the case of regulated companies for the managing director or chief executive to have to be approved in advance before he is appointed. Changes of name, changes of principal office or registered office also sometimes have to be notified in advance. Changes of directors, secretary and various other circumstances also usually have to be notified either immediately or within a stated period after they occur. However, in each case it is necessary to check the regulations concerned. These notifications are of course additional to all the other notifications required under general company law.

27.3 Companies limited by guarantee (charities)

Virtually all the provisions of the Companies Acts which apply to directors of companies limited by shares, also apply to directors of companies limited by guarantee.

In practice, guarantee companies are limited to non-profit making companies and charities.

Charities are frequently set up as companies limited by guarantee rather than as trusts or unincorporated associations. One of the reasons for this is that the charities wish to have limited liability. However as has already been mentioned, limited liability is really something that applies for the benefit of members of a company rather than its directors. In the case of a charitable company limited by guarantee, there is almost always a provision in the memorandum of association which provides that:

> "as regards any property subject to the jurisdiction of the Charity Commissioners for England and Wales or Secretary of State for Education and Science, the governing body of the company shall be chargeable for any such property that may come into their hands and shall be answerable and accountable for their own acts, receipts, neglects and defaults, and for the due administration of such property in the same manner and to the same extent as they would (as such governing body) have been if no incorporation had been effected, and the incorporation of the company shall not diminish or impair any control or authority exercisable by the Chancery Division, the Charity Commissioners or the Secretary of State for Education and Science over such governing body"

As can be seen this provision emphasises that the directors are personally responsible for ensuring that the assets of the charitable company are properly applied for the objects of the charity.

Other aspects of charitable companies which need to be borne in mind are that the members of its governing body can only recover limited expenses from the charity and can only be interested in contracts with the charity to a very limited extent. Also when a charitable company establishes a wholly owned trading subsidiary (which covenants all its profits to the charity) it will usually be provided that no member of the governing body should be an executive or receive remuneration from the trading subsidiary.

Name of charity

Under the Companies Act 1989, if a charity is a company and its name does not include the word "charity" or "charitable", the fact that it is a charity will have to be stated in all business letters, notices, bills of exchange, promissory notes, cheques etc.

Charity's objects

The consent of the Charity Commissioners is required for a charitable company to alter its objects.

APPENDIX A

Standard articles of association

TABLE A

Table A is a standard form of articles of association for a private company which is contained in a statutory instrument. The current version was introduced in 1985, but before that the version in effect dated from 1948 (with some amendments made by later Companies Acts). Table A forms the basis of the articles of association of the vast majority of companies, though often the specific articles of a company will delete or modify provisions of Table A. Public companies often adopt complete forms of articles without reference to Table A, although usually similar or identical in many respects.

The 1948 Table A is still the basis of the articles of many companies, since the 1985 Table A will only apply to companies which have been incorporated or have adopted new articles of association since then. Unless expressly excluded or modified, the form of Table A applying as at the date of a company's incorporation is the version which will constitute the company's articles. *References in the text of this book to standard articles reflect the position as set out in the 1985 Table A (not the 1948 version)*, and care should be taken to check that the position is the same where a company still uses the 1948 Table A. In any event, there is no substitute for carefully checking the articles of association themselves whenever the need arises to check any provision applying to a particular company.

Set out below is a very brief summary of some of the main regulations contained in the 1985 Table A, with cross-references to equivalent or similar provisions of the 1948 version.

1985 TABLE A		1948 TABLE A	
Reg No	Main provisions	**Reg No**	Corresponding provisions noting main variations from 1985 Table A.
Shares			
2	Company may issue shares with any rights or restrictions decided by general meeting.	2	
3	Company may issue redeemable shares.	3	Only redeemable *preference* shares allowed under pre-1981 Table A.
8–11	Company has lien over nil- and partly-paid shares as regards sums due on shares, and powers of sale.	11–14	Lien extends to all debts owing by shareholder under pre-1980 Table A.
12	Company to give 14 clear days' notice of calls for payments on shares.	15	

139

Appendix A

1985 TABLE A		1948 TABLE A	
24	Directors have right to refuse registration of transfer of nil- or partly-paid shares or if procedures not followed.	24	
32	General meeting by ordinary resolution may increase share capital, consolidate or sub-divide shares or cancel unissued shares.	44, 45	
35	Company may purchase own shares, and private company may use capital, subject to Companies Act.		[No such power]

General meetings

38	Notice for general meetings: AGM 21 clear days (or less if all members agree); EGM 14 clear days (or 21 days if special resolution proposed) (or less if majority holding 95% votes agree).	50	
40	Quorum for general meeting: two members (or proxies or corporate representatives).	53	Three members required under pre-1980 Table A.
44	Directors entitled to attend at general meetings.		[No such provision]
46	Resolutions to be decided on show of hands, unless poll (ie record of votes according to rights attaching to shares) demanded by: chairman; two or more members; member holding 1/10 votes or shares equal to 1/10 of paid-up capital.	58	Under pre-1980 Table A, three members (not two) required for demanding a poll.
50	Chairman has a casting vote.	60	

1985 TABLE A		1948 TABLE A	
53	Shareholders' written resolution effective as alternative to general meeting if signatures of all members entitled to vote obtained (on one or more copies of resolution) (*NB* subject to Companies Act requirement for general meeting in exceptional cases).	73A	Only applies to post-1981 Table A. Signatures on more than one copy of resolution not expressly permitted.
55	Jointly held shares: vote of first-named in register of members prevails.	63	
57	No right to votes on shares for which payment due and unpaid.	65	Prohibition extends to votes on *all* shares held if sums unpaid on *any* shares.
60, 62	Appointment of proxy must be in writing and delivered to company at least 48 hours before meeting.	68, 69	

Directors

64	Minimum number of directors: two. No maximum number of directors (subject to any overriding shareholders' ordinary resolution).	75	Number of directors to be determined by subscribers.
65–69	Directors may appoint alternate directors by written notice to company signed by appointor; alternate deemed to be a director for all purposes and may attend and vote at meetings and peform all appointor's functions.		[No equivalent provision].
70	Directors to manage business and exercise all powers of company (subject to Companies Act, other provisions of memorandum and articles and special resolutions).	79, 80	*NB* Directors' authority to exercise company's borrowing powers or charge company's assets subject to maximum equal to amount of issued share capital.

Appendix A

1985 TABLE A		1948 TABLE A	
72	Directors may delegate powers to committee of directors, managing director or other executive director.	102, 109	No express power of delegation to executive directors other than to managing director (or committee of directors)
73–75	1/3 directors to retire at each AGM, by rotation.	89–92	
70, 78	Directors may be appointed by shareholders' ordinary resolution (subject to *either* prior notice, within time limits, by member of intention to propose election *or* recommendation by directors).	93, 94	
79	Directors may themselves appoint a director, but only until next AGM unless then re-appointed.	95	
81	Director vacates office if: prohibited by law from holding office; bankrupt; mental disorder; resigns; six months' unauthorised absence from board meetings and board so resolves.	88	
82, 83	Directors' remuneration determined by shareholders' ordinary resolution, and entitled to expenses properly incurred.	76	
84	Directors have power to appoint managing and other executive directors and determine terms and remuneration.	107–109	Power only applies in respect of managing directors, not other executives.
85, 86	Subject to Companies Act and disclosure to Board of nature and extent of material interests, directors may be interested in transactions with company and retain any benefits received.	84	

Appendix A

	1985 TABLE A		1948 TABLE A
88	Directors may regulate board meetings as they think fit. Any director may call board meeting. Chairman has a casting vote. Directors outside UK not entitled to notice of meetings.	98	
89	Quorum for board meeting: two unless directors decide otherwise)	99	
92	Acts of directors are valid notwithstanding later discovery of default in appointment, or disqualified from holding office or voting, etc.	105	Does not extend to disqualification from voting.
93	Directors' written resolution effective as alternative to board meeting if signatures of all directors entitled to notice of meeting obtained (on one or more copies of resolution).	106	Signatures on more than one copy of resolution not expressly permitted.
94, 95	Director may not vote or count for quorum on any resolution in which he has direct or indirect interest or duty which is material and conflicts or may conflict (with limited exceptions).	84	
Secretary			
99	Secretary to be appointed by, and on terms approved by, and may be removed by, directors.	110	
Seal			
101	Company seal only to be used on authority of directors (or appropriately authorised committee); and sealed documents to be signed by two directors or by one director plus secretary or as otherwise determined by directors.	113	

Appendix A

	1985 TABLE A		1948 TABLE A
Dividends			
102	Dividends to be declared by shareholders' ordinary resolution, subject to recommendation of directors, and subject to Companies Act.	114	
103	Directors may pay interim dividends if justified by profits available for distribution, and subject to Companies Act.	115	
Notices			
111	Any required notices to be in writing, except notices of board meetings.		[No express provision]
118	Subject to Companies Act, director entitled to indemnity by company for cost of court proceedings if judgment given in his favour or acquitted or granted relief by court.	136	

APPENDIX B

Main documents to be filed at Companies Registry

Set out below are the more common matters which are required to be notified to the Registrar of Companies. As to the filing requirements generally, see 17.3 above.

The address to which documents should be sent is:

(for forms relating to changes in share capital)
    Capital Section,
    PO Box 710
    Companies House,
    Cardiff, CF4 3YA

(for forms relating to mortgages or charges)
    Mortgage Section,
    PO Box 716,
    Companies House,
    Cardiff, CF4 3YA

(for most other standard forms)
    General Section,
    Companies House,
    Cardiff, CF4 3UZ.

(for annual returns and accounts, of if in any doubt)
    The Registrar of Companies,
    Companies House,
    Crown Way,
    Maindy,
    Cardiff, CF4 3UZ.

Form Number	Form	Time limit for notification/filing
(i) *Annual return and accounts*		
363	Annual return (giving details of officers, share capital and shareholdings and secured indebtedness as at a specified date)	Not later than 12 months after the previous annual return form
—	Annual audited accounts	7 months (public companies), 10 months (private companies) after end of accounting period
224	Notice of company's first accounting reference date	6 months from incorporation

225(1)	A change of accounting reference date	Before end of accounting reference period to be amended

(ii) Registered office

287	A change of registered office	14 days

(iii) Directors and secretary

288	A change in the directors or secretary or in any of their registered details	14 days

(iv) Share capital

123	An increase of the company's authorised share capital	15 days
88(2)	An allotment of shares	1 month
122	Changes to share capital (including consolidation, division or sub-division and redemption or cancellation)	1 month

(v) Charges

395	A charge over the company's property or undertaking	21 days
403A	Discharge of mortgage or charge	—

(vi) Resolutions

	The undermentioned resolutions need to be filed (there is no special form which needs to be used): (i) special resolutions (ii) extraordinary resolutions (iii) resolutions or agreements agreed to by all the members but which would not have been effective unless passed as special or extraordinary resolutions. (iv) resolutions or agreements binding members of a class of shares (v) elective resolutions or resolutions revoking them (vi) resolution relating to authority of directors to issue shares (vii) resolution relating to authority for market purchase of company's own shares (viii) resolution for voluntary winding-up	15 days

(ix) *Memorandum and articles of association*

If a special resolution is passed altering either the memorandum of association or the articles of association then a copy of the memorandum of association or the articles of association (as the case may be) needs to be filed incorporating the change.

15 days

Index

	Para
Accounts	
advance corporation tax,	16.8
audited,	
error in,	16.6
filing of,	23.2
latest,	1.10
requirement for,	16.3
auditors,	16.5
corporation tax,	16.7
management,	16.2
records, duty to keep,	16.1
time limit for laying and filing,	16.4
Action. *See* Litigation	
Acts of others	
responsibility for,	5.4
Adjournments,	23.8
Administration	
company,	
documents,	17.4
seal,	17.7
secretary,	17.6
stationery,	17.4
documents,	
availability for inspection,	17.1
Companies House, filing at,	17.3
company,	17.4
places of business,	17.5
records,	17.1
statutory books,	17.2
Advance corporation tax,	16.8
Agreement	
shareholders,	1.12
Alternate directors	3.4
Annual general meeting,	23.1
Annual return,	23.2
Appointment of director	
check list of steps taken,	4.2
employment contract,	4.3
how made,	4.1
Arrangements subject to restriction	
general,	11.1
loans to directors,	11.3
loss of office, compensation for,	11.5
retirement, payments as compensation on,	11.5
service contracts,	11.2
substantial property transactions,	11.4
See also Disclosure of interests	

	Para
Articles of association	
checking,	1.9
liability, exemption from,	7.3
limited company,	2.4
Assets	
company, duty not to mis-apply,	6.8
Attention	
duty relating to,	5.3
Audited accounts. *See* Accounts	
Auditors,	16.5
Authorised share capital,	18.2
Authority to issue shares,	18.4
Bank	
accounts,	9.10
cheques,	9.10
Benefits	
general considerations,	13.1
pensions,	13.4
See also Remuneration	
Bills of exchange	
liability for,	14.8
Board	
meetings. *See* Board meetings	
power of,	
exceeding,	9.3
generally,	9.1
Board meetings	
attendance at,	5.3
chairman,	8.8
committees,	8.13
decisions,	8.9
delegation,	8.13
dissent,	8.14
frequency of,	8.3
general conduct,	8.4
minutes,	
circulation of,	8.12
generally,	8.11
need for,	8.1
notice of,	8.5
quorum,	
difficulty obtaining,	8.7
generally,	8.6
voting where director has interest,	8.10
written resolutions,	8.2
Books	
statutory,	17.2

Para

Borrowing
   Powers relating to,   9.9
Business
   places of,   17.5

Capital
   share. *See* Shares
Care
   director's duty of,   3.5, 5.2
Cash
   issues of shares for,   18.6
Ceasing to be director
   activities,
      after leaving,   26.9
      prior to leaving,   26.8
   compensation,   26.6
   disqualification,   26.3
   executive director, dismissal of,   26.5
   formalities,   26.7
   removal,   26.4
   resignation,   26.1
   retirement. *See* Retirement
   rights on removal from office,   26.6
Certificates
   share,   18.10, 21.4
Chairman,   8.8
Charges
   powers relating to,   9.9
Charity
   guarantee company,   27.3
   name of,   27.3
   objects,   27.3
Cheques,   9.10
Circulars,   22.4
Circulation of minutes,   8.12
Class meetings,   23.4
Close companies,   16.7
Collateral purpose
   duty not to exercise powers for,   6.3
Committees
   board meeting, delegation by,   8.13
Community
   duty to,   5.8
Companies Act offences
   liability for,   14.5
Companies House
   filing documents at,   17.3, App B
Company
   activities after leaving,   26.9
   articles of association,   1.9
   assets, duty not to mis-apply,   6.8
   best interests of, duty to act in,   6.2
   close,   16.7
   documents,   17.4
   exceeding powers of,   9.3
   guarantee, limited by,   27.3
   latest audited accounts,   1.10

Para

   limited. *See* Limited company
   listed,   1.11, 27.1
   memorandum,   1.9
   name, restriction on re-use of,   15.11
   private. *See* Private company
   public, transfer of shares,   21.3
   regulated,   27.2
   seal,   17.7
   secretary,   17.6
   shares. *See* Shares
   stationery,   17.4
   subsidiaries,   1.11, 27.1
   third parties, statutory protection
      given to,   9.5
Compensation
   loss of office, for,   11.5
   removal from office, rights on,   26.6
   retirement, on,   11.5
Competition
   duties relating to,   6.4
Conduct
   board meetings, of,   8.4
   shareholders' meetings, of,   23.6
Confidentiality
   duty of,   6.5
Conflicts,   1.8
Consideration. *See* Cash
Consumers
   duty to,   5.8
Contract
   employment,   4.3
   liability for,   14.2
   liability, exemption from,   7.3
   service,   11.2
   subject to,   25.3
Corporation tax
   advance,   16.8
   close companies,   16.7
   liability for,   16.7
   payment of,   16.7
   rate of,   16.7
Court
   relief from liability by,   7.2
Creditors
   duty to,   5.7
Criminal offences
   liability for,   14.4

Decisions of board meetings,   8.9
Delegation
   board meeting, by,   8.13
   duty relating to,   5.4
Disclosure of interests
   duty relating to,   6.6
   effect of,   10.5
   general interests,   10.3
   generally,   10.2

Index

	Para		Para
nature of interests disclosed,	10.4	Expenses,	13.2, 13.5
shareholders, ratification by,	10.6	Extraordinary general meetings,	23.3
Discovery,	25.4		
Dismissal of executive director,	26.5	Fees,	13.2
Disqualification of director,	15.10, 26.3	Fiduciary duties. *See* Duties of director	
Dissent,	8.14		
Dividends		Finance	
payment of,	9.8	problems, steps to take when arising,	15.5
Documents		shares, assistance for acquisition of. *See* Shares	
Companies House, filing at,	17.3, App B	Formalities	
company,	17.4	ceasing to be director,	26.7
inspection, availability for,	17.1	share issue, in respect of,	18.9
Duties of director		Fraudulent trading	
fiduciary,		consequences of,	15.2
best interests of company, duty to act in,	6.2	general precautions to take in advance,	15.4
collateral purpose, duty not to exercise powers for,	6.3	Frequency of meetings,	8.3
company assets, duty not to mis-apply,	6.8	General duties. *See* Duties of director	
competition, relating to,	6.4	Gratuitous transactions,	9.7
confidentiality,	6.5	Guarantee	
disclosure of interests,	6.6	company limited by,	27.3
general,	6.1	liability for,	14.7
nominee directors,	6.9		
secret profits, duty not to make,	6.7	Independence,	1.3
general,		Information,	1.5
acts of others, responsibility for,	5.4	Insider dealing,	12.3
attention,	5.3	Insolvency	
best interests of company, acting in,	3.5	company name, restrictions on re-use of,	15.11
board meetings, attendance at,	5.3	disqualification of directors,	15.10
care and skill,	3.5, 5.2	financial problems, commencement of,	15.5
community, duty to,	5.8	fraudulent trading,	15.2
consumers, duty to,	5.8	general precautions,	15.4
creditors, duty to,	3.5, 5.7	generally,	15.1
delegation,	5.4	liquidation,	
honesty,	3.5	methods,	15.8
interests of employees, duty to have regard to,	5.6	position once inevitable,	15.7
position, duty not to abuse,	3.5	misfeasance,	15.9
powers, duty not to exceed,	5.5	transactions on becoming insolvent,	15.6
statutory obligations,	3.5, 5.9	wrongful trading,	15.3
time,	5.3	Inspection	
variety of,	5.1	documents and records available for,	17.1
Elective resolutions,	24.5	Insurance	
Employees		liability, relief from,	7.6
interests of, duty to have regard to,	5.6	Interests	
Employment contract,	4.3	company, of, duty to act in,	6.2
Errors		disclosure of. *See* Disclosure of interests	
audited accounts, in,	16.6		
Executive director		employees, of, duty to have regard to,	5.6
dismissal of,	26.5	generally,	10.1
Executives			
remuneration as,	13.3		

Para

Interests—*continued*
  share, notification of, 12.1
  voting where director has, 8.10

Issue of shares. *See* Shares

Liability
  acts of others, for, 5.4
  bills of exchange, for, 14.8
  Companies Act offences, for, 14.5
  contract, for, 14.2
  corporation tax, for, 16.7
  criminal offences, for, 14.4
  general position, 14.1
  guarantees, for, 14.7
  negligence, for, 14.3
  other, 14.9
  relief from,
    court, by, 7.2
    general, 7.1
    insurance, 7.6
    ratification, 7.5
    settlement of claim, 7.4
  shares, financial assistance for acquisition of, 19.4
  tax, for, 14.6
  tort, for, 14.3

Limitation
  actions, of, 25.6
  powers, of, 9.2

Limited company
  articles of association, 2.4
  distinguishing features, 2.1
  formation of, 2.2
  memorandum of association, 2.3
  nature of, 1.1
  shareholders and directors, relationship between, 2.7
  third parties, safeguards for, 2.6
  types of, 2.5

Liquidation
  methods, 15.8
  position once inevitable, 15.7
  See also Insolvency

Listed companies, 1.11, 27.1

Litigation
  action to take, 25.5
  discovery, 25.4
  limitation of actions, 25.6
  outline of proceedings, 25.1
  subject to contract, 25.3
  without prejudice, 25.3
  written records, importance of, 25.2

Loans to director, 11.3

Loss of office
  compensation for, 11.5

Management accounts, 16.2

Para

Meetings
  board. *See* Board meetings
  shareholders. *See* Shareholders

Memorandum of association
  checking, 1.9
  limited company, 2.3

Minority rights, 22.7

Minutes
  board meetings, of, 8.11, 8.12
  circulation of, 8.12
  shareholders' meetings, of, 23.9

Misfeasance, 15.9

Misuse of directors' powers, 9.6

Name
  charity, of, 27.3
  company, restrictions on re-use of, 15.11

Negligence
  liability for, 14.3

Nominee directors, 6.9

Non-cash consideration
  issue of shares for, 18.7

Notice of meetings, 8.5

Number of directors, 3.6

Offences
  Companies Act, 14.5
  criminal, 14.4

Office
  ceasing to hold. *See* Ceasing to be director
  compensation for loss of, 11.5

Payments as compensation, 11.5

Pensions, 13.4

Places of business, 17.5

Powers of director
  bank accounts, 9.10
  board, of,
    exceeding, 9.3
    generally, 9.1
  borrowing, relating to, 9.9
  charges, relating to, 9.9
  cheques, 9.10
  company, of, exceeding, 9.3
  dividends, payment of, 9.8
  duty not to exceed, 5.5
  gratuitous transactions, 9.7
  individual director, of, 9.4
  limitation of, 9.2
  misuse of, 9.6
  third parties, statutory protection given to, 9.5

Pre-emption rights, 18.5

	Para
Private company	
own shares, financial assistance for	
acquisition of,	19.3
purchase of own shares,	20.3
redeemable shares,	20.3
resolutions,	
elective,	24.5
statutory written,	24.4
transfer of shares,	21.3
Proceedings. *See* Litigation	
Profits	
secret, duty not to make,	6.7
Property transactions,	11.4
Prospectuses,	22.5
Proxies,	23.7
Public company	
transfer of shares,	21.3
Purchase of own shares. *See* Shares	
Qualifications,	1.6
Quorum	
board meetings, at,	8.6, 8.7
difficulty obtaining,	8.7
Ratification	
liability, relief from,	7.5
shareholders, by,	10.6
Records	
accounting, duty to keep,	16.1
inspection, availability for,	17.1
written, importance of,	25.2
Redeemable shares,	20.2, 20.3
Regulated companies,	27.2
Relief from liability. *See* Liability	
Removal of director,	26.4, 26.6
Remuneration	
executives, as,	13.3
expenses,	13.2, 13.5
fees,	13.2
general considerations,	13.1
pensions,	13.4
taxation,	13.7
Resignation,	26.1
Resolutions	
amendments to,	24.2
elective,	24.5
statutory written,	24.4
types of,	24.1
written,	8.2, 24.3, 24.4
Responsibilities,	1.2
Restrictions,	1.7
Retirement	
payments as compensation on,	11.5
rotation, by,	26.2
Role of director,	3.1

	Para
Seal,	17.7
Secret profits	
duty not to make,	6.7
Secretary of company,	17.6
Service contract,	11.2
Settlement of claim,	7.4
Shadow directors,	3.3
Shareholders	
agreement,	1.12
approval,	
dealings which require,	22.2
other,	22.3
circulars,	22.4
general duties of,	22.1
limited company, of, relationship	
with directors,	2.7
meetings,	
adjournments,	23.8
annual general,	23.1
annual return,	23.2
audited accounts, filing of,	23.2
calling,	23.5
class,	23.4
conduct of,	23.6
extraordinary general,	23.3
minutes,	23.9
proxies,	23.7
minority rights,	22.7
prospectuses,	22.5
ratification by,	10.6
resolutions,	
amendments to,	24.2
elective,	24.5
statutory written,	24.4
types of,	24.1
written,	24.3
takeovers,	22.6
Shares	
capital,	
authorised,	18.2
reduction of,	20.4
certificates,	18.10, 21.4
financial assistance for acquisition of,	
general exceptions,	19.2
general prohibition,	19.1
liability of directors,	19.4
private companies,	19.3
insider dealing,	12.3
interests in company, notification	
of,	12.1
issue of,	
authorised share capital,	18.2
authority for,	18.4
cash, for,	18.6
certificates,	18.10
directors' duties in respect of,	18.8
formalities in respect of,	18.9

Para

Shares—*continued*
    general, 18.1
    non-cash consideration, for, 18.7
    pre-emption rights, 18.5
    types of shares, 18.3
    options, dealing in, 12.2
    purchase by company of own,
        market purchase, 20.1
        off-market purchase, 20.1
        private company, 20.3
        tax, 20.5
    redeemable, 20.2, 20.3
    schemes, 13.6
    transfer of,
        form of, 21.2
        general, 21.1
        pre-emption rights, 21.3
        restrictions on, 21.3
        share certificates, 21.4
    types of, 18.3
Skill
    director's duty of, 3.5, 5.2
Stationery
    company, 17.4
Statutory books, 17.2
Statutory obligations, 3.5, 5.9
Statutory written resolutions, 24.4
Subject to contract, 25.3
Subsidiary companies, 1.11, 27.1
Substantial property transactions, 11.4

Table A
    important provisions in, App A
Takeovers, 22.6
Taxation
    liability for, 14.6

Para

    purchase by company of own
        shares, 20.5
    remuneration, of, 13.7
    See also Corporation tax
Third parties
    acts of, responsibility for, 5.4
    limited liability, safeguards relating
        to, 2.6
    statutory protection given to, 9.5
Time
    accounts, limit for laying and
        filing, 16.4
    consideration of, 1.4
    duty relating to, 5.3
Tort
    liability for, 14.3
Trading
    fraudulent, 15.2
    wrongful, 15.3
Transactions
    gratuitous, 9.7
    insolvency, on, 15.6
    property, 11.4
Transfer of shares. *See* Shares

Voting
    director having interest, where, 8.10

Who is director, 3.2
Without prejudice, 25.3
Written resolutions, 8.2, 24.3, 24.4
Wrongful trading
    general precautions to take in
        advance, 15.4
    when arising, 15.3